THE SEARCH
FOR A STYLE

THE SEARCH FOR A STYLE

COUNTRY LIFE AND ARCHITECTURE 1897-1935

JOHN CORNFORTH

W.W. Norton & Company

New York · London

Other books by John Cornforth

✳

English Country Houses: Caroline
(with Oliver Hill)

The Country Houses of Britain: Can They Survive?

English Decoration in the Eighteenth Century
(with John Fowler)

The Quest for Comfort: English Interiors 1790–1818

The Inspiration of the Past

Copyright © 1988 by John Cornforth
First American Edition, 1989

All Rights Reserved
Originally published in the United Kingdom by
André Deutsch Limited, 1988

Library of Congress Cataloging-in-Publication Data

The Search for a style: Country life and architecture, 1897-1935/
John Cornforth.
    p.   cm.
  1. Country houses—England—Themes, motives.   2. Manors—England—
—Themes, motives.   3. Interior decoration—England—Themes, motives.
4. England—Social life and customs.   5. Country life—England.
I. Cornforth, John, 1937—.   II. Country life (London, England)
NA7562.S43,   1988
728.8'0942—dc19   89–3144

ISBN 0-393-02703-1

W.W. Norton & Company, Inc., 500 Fifth Avenue, New York, NY 10110
W.W. Norton & Company, Ltd., 37 Great Russell Street, London WC1B 3NU

Printed in Italy
1 2 3 4 5 6 7 8 9 0

CONTENTS

Preface · *6*

PART ONE

1 · Country Life: Country Homes · *12*
2 · Enthusiasms and Opportunities · *18*
3 · People and Places · *37*

PART TWO

The English Interior
Through the Eyes of Country Life · *87*

Index of the Houses Illustrated · 262
General Index · 263

PREFACE

In 1976 Nicholas Cooper produced *The Opulent Eye*, an evocative selection of photographs of late Victorian and Edwardian interiors taken by Bedford Lemere, that I enjoyed at the time and have frequently referred to again. Since then the Lutyens exhibition at the Hayward Gallery in 1981/82, Clive Aslet's book *The Last Country Houses* (1982), my own *Inspiration of the Past* (1985), as well as the ninetieth birthday of *Country Life* in January 1987, have led me to look at a great number of old photographs in the magazine, and they prompted me to attempt a Country Life equivalent to *The Opulent Eye*.

This book, however, and a hoped-for sequel, cover a longer period, and in the introductory essay the aim is to show how the visual chronicle relates not only to *Country Life's* interest in houses and architecture and those people who were involved in its development, but also to certain aspects of the history of taste. On the other hand no attempt is made to give an account of the development of architecture, domestic or otherwise.

The period covered is from the foundation of *Country Life* in 1897 to 1935, a date that needs explanation. I have chosen it, because it is close to the half-way point in *Country Life's* history up to now and it reached its 2000th number on May 18, 1935. Moreover, it is close to the deaths of the founder of the magazine, Edward Hudson, in 1936, and of H. Avray Tipping, who established the tradition of architectural writing, in 1933. Also it marked a caesura in the interests of Christopher Hussey: by then he had been at *Country Life* for fourteen years – and he was to remain involved for another thirty-five – but in the mid 1930s he lost confidence in the way architecture was going and in his hope for a synthesis of old and new that would produce a satisfactory style for his generation.

That in turn linked up with a new interest in the preservation of unspoiled landscape and historic architecture, which found particular expression in the National Trust's Country Houses Scheme and the establishment of the Georgian Group in 1937.

There is no proper history of *Country Life*, (although Bernard Darwin wrote a short account that was privately printed in 1947) and it has kept no archives. Nor apparently are there papers that relate to Edward Hudson, or to its architectural writers before Christopher Hussey. Christopher Hussey's own papers are uneven: while he kept many reminders of his early life, there is surprisingly little that throws light on his long involvement with *Country Life*.

There are, however, a number of articles that are useful pointers by, among others, H. Avray Tipping, Lawrence Weaver and Christopher Hussey (see page 9). Richard Haslam has written two on Tipping's houses. Also I have written three pairs of articles about Christopher Hussey, an essay about 'Country Life and Lutyens' for the catalogue of the exhibition of 1981/82 and also a forthcoming essay about 'Lawrence Weaver and Country Life'. For some time I have wanted to tie those fragments together and develop them, but such is the nature of the material that I believe it is more suited to the long essay introducing this book than to a book in itself.

Its backbone is, obviously, the series of articles of which the full title is *Country Homes and Gardens Old and New*, but I decided at the outset that *Homes* and *Gardens* should be separated. *Country Life's* treatment of gardens deserved a companion book, or books, which I am not competent to write.

The text of the present book falls into two parts, the essay being followed by notes on the illustrations. These, it is hoped, will not only suggest the approach of the authors of the original articles but also the mood of the houses and the way attitudes to some of them have changed since the articles were written.

The choice of illustrations is slanted in favour of new interiors and restorations, rather than the more frequently reproduced views of great rooms in famous houses, many of which have appeared in recent years in Christopher Hussey's trilogy on Georgian country houses and their companion volumes. Also I have omitted as far as possible illustrations that I included in *The Inspiration of the Past*, even if that has meant not always choosing the key view of an interior on this occasion.

A Note on the Illustrations

Since this is primarily a picture book, and a picture book of old photographs, a brief note on the illustrations is called for. No one outside *Country Life* would believe the work involved in producing such a series of illustrations from the photographic library. Looking out the glass negatives in the thousands of boxes is a daunting and often frustrating, as well as a dusty, task. Many negatives have individual numbers but there is no subject index listing each negative; and the card index of jobs has numbers, but usually no dates. So it can be a case of hunting for a needle in a haystack. I am very grateful to Camilla Costelloe, the librarian, for helping me over this, and even more grateful to her for putting all the negatives away again.

Trevor Woods, who has worked in the photographic studio since he joined *Country Life* twenty-seven years ago, has done a splendid job in printing them up. That was an even more formidable task. Virtually all the negatives had to be cleaned by hand to remove the silver off the surface of the plates. Then there is no machine capable of taking the 12 inch by 10 inch glass negatives, so they have to be contact-printed on a baseboard. Often several prints have to be taken, like states of an etching, in order to get the balance of the tones right. That involves a combination of hand and eye, increasing light in some areas and cutting it back in others through using 'dodgers' (sheets of paper specially cut for each negative and held in a wire over the baseboard). Also, because the negatives tend to be too contrasty for the softest paper available today, the paper has to be 'pre-flashed' first to fog it, and so reduce the contrast.

Inevitably over the years a number of the glass negatives have been broken, or at least damaged. Some of the photographs were taken for

Country Life rather than by staff photographers, so those negatives do not exist. Others have strayed, so that there are disappointments – and also unexpected rewards when a negative appears in the wrong box. When a negative is missing there are two alternatives: to rephotograph an old print, if one exists in the files, or (less satisfactory) to rephotograph an illustration in the magazine and then work from a copy negative.

As far as possible the illustrations have been printed from new prints from the negatives; a few are printed from existing old prints, while others, which I have indicated in the text, have had to be printed from copy negatives. Such an explanation is only fair to Charles Latham, A.E. Henson and their colleagues, and also to Trevor Woods.

Author's Note and Acknowledgements

The idea of this book came to me after a discussion with Michael Wright, then publisher of *Country Life*; and it was his positive response to my half-developed idea and his constructive agreement with the publishers that has made it possible. So to him I am doubly grateful.

Past and present members of the staff of *Country Life* have also helped me, in particular Fred Harden, whose memory goes back no less than sixty-six years, Dorothy Stroud, Alex Starkey who happily is still there after thirty-three years, and Clive Aslet who has been there a mere ten but who is particularly interested in new houses of the period. Miss Maudie Henson has provided information about her father, A.E. Henson. I would also like to thank Mrs Christopher Hussey, who encouraged me to use Christopher Hussey's papers for earlier articles about his life and work, and his friends and contemporaries who helped when I was writing them.

Among others who have helped me in various ways are Colin Amery, Major Congreve, Dan Cruickshank, John Hardy and John Harris, the last of whom read the text, knowing the pictures.

At André Deutsch Diana Athill had the daunting task of grappling with the text while not knowing the pictures, an act of faith, before being faced with a 'dummy' bulging with photocopies; while Behram Kapadia was faced with turning the said 'dummy', plus a flood of photographs, into an intelligible, elegant layout.

The houses illustrated are listed in alphabetical order at the end of the book, separately from the index of people and publications.

A book of pictures with an introductory essay should not be weighed down with footnotes and references, but because of the nature of this one, a chronological list of publications that throw light on it is called for, if only to help the few hunting for them in the haystack of *Country Life*.

AUTHOR'S NOTE AND ACKNOWLEDGEMENTS

Country Life, March 4, 1916: 'The Country Homes of England as Revealed in a Thousand Numbers', H.A. Tipping

Country Life, January 7, 1922: 'Country Life's Five and Twentieth Birthday'

Country Life, March 28, 1925: Obituary of Percy Macquoid by H.A. Tipping

Lawrence Weaver by Clough Williams-Ellis (1933)

Country Life, November 25, 1933: 'The late H.Avray Tipping. A Personal Recollection' by Lady Congreve; 'Gardener and Antiquary' by Christopher Hussey

Country Life, May 18, 1935: 'The Country Houses of England: a Retrospect of 2000 Numbers' by Christopher Hussey

Country Life, September 26, 1936: 'Edward Hudson' by Christopher Hussey

Scaffolding in the Sky by C.H. Reilly (1938)

Fifty Years of Country Life by Bernard Darwin (1947)

'Photogrametry in the Restoration of Castle Howard' by E.H. Thompson, *The Photogrametric Record*, Vol IX No 20, October, 1962

Country Life, January 12, 1967: 'Early Treatment of Country Houses' by Christopher Hussey; 'Edward Hudson, the Founder of Country Life' by Pamela Maude

'Christopher Hussey: a Bibliographical Tribute' by J.M. Crook, *Architectural History XIII* (1970)

'Percy Macquoid and Others' by Ralph Edwards, *Apollo*, May, 1974

Country Life, May 10 and 17, 1979: 'The Husseys and the Picturesque' by John Cornforth

Country Life, December 6, 13, 1979: 'The Houses of H.Avray Tipping' by Richard Haslam

The Rise of Architectural History by David Watkin (1980)

Country Life, October 22 and 29, 1981: 'Christopher Hussey and Modern Architecture' by John Cornforth

'Lutyens and Country Life: 81 Not Out' by John Cornforth: essay in the catalogue of the Lutyens exhibition, 1981

'Percy Macquoid' by Donald Beevers, *Antique Collector*, June and July, 1984

Country Life, January 8, 1987: 'Balancing Past and Present: the Country House Between the Wars' by John Cornforth

PART ONE

Country Life;
Country Homes

1. *Baddesley Clinton, Warwickshire. The first photograph of a country house to appear in*
Country Life *on January 1, 1897 (reproduced from a copy negative)*

Chapter 1

COUNTRY LIFE: COUNTRY HOMES

I f the twentieth century looks at seventeenth-century country houses and gardens through the engraved bird's-eyes of Kip, and at the romantic taste of the early nineteenth century through the lithographic plates of Nash's *Mansions of England in the Olden Time*, the twenty-first century will surely interpret the twentieth-century approach to country houses through the photographs taken for Country Life over the past ninety years. That is not just because so many have been published, but because a succession of photographers have looked at houses and gardens in a particular way. When their work appears elsewhere, it invariably stands out as having a 'Country Life' look, because of the composition of the photographs, their still, even lighting and the clarity of detail.

The particular style of *Country Life* photographs came over particularly strongly in the exhibition devoted to Lutyens in 1981, which included so many of them. However, as far as I am aware, no one has attempted to analyse the possible importance of photography to Lutyens, both as a way of looking at buildings and as a source of ideas. Going through old volumes of Country Life has made me wonder about the extent to which, consciously or unconsciously, he and other architects absorbed ideas seen in the magazine into their processes of design. For instance, was it knowledge of the arcade in the Marble Parlour at Houghton (fig. 166) as illustrated in *Country Life* in 1921 that inspired the Semi-State Dining room at Viceroys House in Delhi (fig. 229) and the dining room at Gledstone, (fig. 260) and were the vaulted corridors in Delhi (fig. 228) at least partly inspired by the corridors at Castle Howard (fig. 199)?

Certainly photography, and *Country Life* photography in particular, has influenced the arrangement of rooms, encouraging for example the removal of groups of miscellaneous furniture of the kind seen in the library at Sledmere in 1897 (fig. 50). This was done partly out of a desire to show the form of a room and its principal features as clearly as possible, as can be seen when the first photograph of the Saloon at Nostell Priory (fig. 99), published in 1907 before Adam's architecture and decoration was appreciated, is compared with the second one published in 1914 (fig. 2), when Arthur Bolton wrote his article in connection with his book intended to restore the Adams' reputation.

Because the influence of *Country Life* photography is undeniable, it

2. The saloon at Nostell Priory, Yorkshire, in 1914. By then the Victorian clutter shown in the photograph taken in 1907 (Fig 99) had been removed and the purity of the Adam design re-emphasised

seemed worth examining how its vision was created and how it developed in its first thirty-eight years. Many of the best photographs are still taken on a plate camera made by Gandolfi, and at least one of the lenses used by Alex Starkey, who has been at *Country Life* for thirty-five years, was used by his predecessor, A.E. Henson, over sixty years ago.

Country Life is supposed to have been conceived on the golf course at Walton Heath, in Surrey, and the place and the date, about 1895 or 96, are both more appropriate than might be imagined. It was the brain child of Edward Hudson and George Riddell. Hudson was a prosperous London business man, whose family firm, Hudson and Kearns, were printers and blockmakers already concerned with the still relatively new illustrated magazines trade. George Riddell was a solicitor, who was legal adviser to *The News of the World* and a power in George Newnes Limited, publishers of magazines. (Later he was knighted, made a baronet and finally created Lord Riddell of Walton Heath.) As Bernard Darwin explained in his *Fifty Years of Country Life*, they wanted 'a weekly illustrated paper of the highest quality that would get the best possible results from half-tone blocks'.

If to a later generation *Country Life* and *The News of the World* would appear to have little in common, at least Lord Riddell enjoyed the contrast, as C.H. Reilly recalled in his autobiography *Scaffolding in the Sky* (1938). He had invited Riddell to visit the School of Architecture at Liverpool, where he 'gave his *Country Life* side in opening the exhibition in the afternoon, and his *News of the World* one at the University Club in the evening. I remember his saying, "What will the Recording Angel think of me owning two such different papers? What different views of the British race he must get from them. From *Country Life* he would gather the British were a race of decadent aesthetes only interested in the cult of their ancestors, but from *The News of the World* he would think – What a virile people, always raping and murdering each other." '

Edward Hudson was already collaborating with George Newnes in the publication of *Navy and Army Illustrated*, and Newnes was building up his publishing empire. His first great success had been with *Tit Bits*, an ancestor of *Playboy*, which he started in Manchester in 1881. Three years later he transferred his business to London, founding *The Strand Magazine* in 1891 and *The Pall Mall Gazette*, an evening daily paper, in 1892. Both he and Hudson wanted to expand, Hudson being keen to make fuller use of his printing facilities, and in 1897 Newnes reconstructed his company, increasing its capital to £1m.

Not long before that he and Hudson had acquired *Racing Illustrated*, a not very successful paper, and on January 1, 1897, they relaunched it as *Country Life Illustrated*, price 6d. It was a joint venture, and, when eight years later *Country Life* was made into a separate company, the shares were held equally by Hudson and Newnes' interests. The editorial office was in Tavistock Street, Covent Garden, while the advertising and publishing was handled from Newnes's offices round the corner in Southampton Street.

The revamped magazine was based on down-to-earth commercial sense and ambition: its general character and its advertising were directed at readers who might well be members of a Surrey golf club. Good trains to London and more reliable motor cars provided new opportunities for the prosperous middle classes to build houses in the still unspoiled rural landscape, and enjoy the conventional pleasures of country life, gardening, riding and golf.

Country Life's distinctive character, however, seems to have been largely a reflection of Edward Hudson's own enthusiasms. All who remember him agree that he was an inarticulate man who found expression through his magazine. According to one account he became interested in country houses through taking his delicate elder brother for drives, but, according to Ralph Edwards, Hudson himself said that 'as a printer's traveller for the family firm, he "fell" for the country houses of which he caught glimpses through the park gates; taking a bicycle with him expressly to see them. It struck him suddenly what a subject for a paper.'

Although his family was prosperous, he had had little formal education, having left school at fifteen to be articled to a solicitor. He soon proved himself to be both able and determined, becoming chief conveyancing clerk of his firm by the time he was seventeen. When he was twenty-one, he persuaded his father to let him take over the family business. He had to teach himself about buildings and history and develop what must have been a natural eye and an innate romantic sympathy for the past as he went along. When he got the idea of *Country Life Illustrated*, he was still feeling his way forward step by step, and it says a great deal for his intuition that he got the blend of material right.

From the very beginning there was an article on an old house. The first one was Baddesley Clinton in Warwickshire (fig. 1), but that was a very tentative exercise extending to just over two pages with a couple

*3. The decorative headpiece by
J. Byam Shaw introduced on
January 8, 1898*

of photographs and a single page of text written by John Leyland. In the following weeks there were articles on three neighbouring places, Charlecote Park, Warwick Castle and Guys Cliff, the choice being presumably dictated by the travels of the photographer. Also there were articles on the stud at Sledmere and – almost as an afterthought – one on the house that included views of the South Hall and the library taken by W.A. Rouch, a blood-stock photographer. They were the first interiors (figs. 49, 50) to appear in the magazine. Next, on May 8, 1897, came a photograph of the King James Drawing Room at Hatfield (fig. 51), but its quality was not very high: It is evident that Hudson had not yet found a suitable photographer.

Moreover there were considerable problems in photographing interiors arising from the need for artificial lighting. The only alternative to very long exposures was to use flash powder made of magnesium, which was messy and as dangerous as indoor fireworks.

Early the following year, the whole concept of the articles became more organised, as can be seen from the new decorative headpiece by J. Byam Shaw (fig. 3), apparently inspired by Walter Crane's *The Decorative Illustration of Books* (1896), and the embracing title *Country Homes and Gardens Old and New*. About the same time Charles Latham, who was already established as an architectural photographer, began to work for the magazine. The emphasis was still on exteriors and gardens, although interiors were included as well, and it was only after about four years that a better balance was struck.

By 1904, however, the magazine had become established and had won the respect of serious commentators including Muthesius, an architect attached to the German Embassy from 1896 to 1903. He wrote in a section of *The English House* called 'New Move to the Country', 'For the past ten years there has been a very active market towards a close contact with nature. A number of excellent journals (e.g. *Country Life* begun 1897) dealing in detail with every thing connected with life in the country have begun publication. There has been a great increase recently in trips into the country, especially those that last from Saturday to Monday . . . preference for types of sport (e.g. golf) that necessitate a stay in the open country; and finally a great love of gardens.'

It is not surprising that *Country Life's* beginning was hesitant, when the magazine was intended to cover such a broad field and the people behind it were commercial men trying to work out a profitable idea, rather than enthusiasts with a definite concept seeking commercial backing. Technical developments in printing coincided with new possibilities

4. *Knight, Frank and Rutley's first full page advertisement in* Country Life *on August 27, 1898*

of creating a readership and attracting advertising; but even so Hudson and Riddell would not have caught the mood of the time unless they had been skilful as well as lucky.

That is apparent, for instance, in their approach to property advertising, which has always been an integral part of the paper and arguably more widely studied than the Country Homes articles themselves. Clearly they realised that there was considerable commercial potential, and it cannot be just coincidence that the firm of Knight Frank and Rutley started business in April, 1896. As Alan Jenkins has written in *Men of Property*, a history of that firm, 'Hudson glamorized the country , made successful business men long to live in it, secure in the knowledge that by selling up and buying land one could become at least a sort of gentleman. From its outset Howard Frank cultivated a special relationship with *Country Life*, paying record prices for key advertising positions. A landmark was Howard Frank's first full-page in the magazine (fig. 4) (27 August 1898), resplendent with photographs.'

Quite apart from being commercial, the property advertising has also always been part of the pipe-dream aspect of English life presented by *Country Life*. All over the world people regularly follow the magazine in order to pick their house of the week, even though they have no intention of living in England. For some the pipe-dream becomes an unexpected reality. So it was with Arthur Lee, Viscount Lee of Fareham, who wrote in the 2000th number of *Country Life* on May 18, 1935: 'In January, 1897, when serving in Canada, I was turning over the newly arrived English papers in the Montreal Club and was thrilled to come across a new weekly journal of which the outstanding feature, as it seemed to me, was an intoxicating array of temptations in the shape of English country houses – Tudor, Jacobean, Georgian and what not – which were at the disposal of any homesick exile who could make a fortune overseas and retire to his native land. From that time I indulged weekly and with the growing fervour of a hopeless passion, in the dream of my 'Castle in Spain' which eventually led me to stumble upon Chequers (figs. 118, 119) at a time when I was really in search of a week-end cottage on the Thames.'

The growth in property advertising was related to the break up of estates that followed the agricultural slump of the 1870s, the passing of the Settled Land Act of 1882, which gave tenants for life power to sell land, and the introduction of death duties in 1894. In the late 1880s there had not been much demand for land, and, as a writer in *The Times* stated in 1887, capitalists preferred to rent rather than buy land for sport and distrusted it as an investment. Thus many large houses to let are to be found in the early advertisement pages of *Country Life*, among them Knole, as an unnamed house convenient for London, with the Great Hall set out for luncheon at a series of round tables.

The growth in the property pages in *Country Life* can be directly related to the growth of the market, and again that can be illustrated from the history of Knight Frank and Rutley, whose property sales quadrupled between 1903 and 1909. However, it was not until 1912 that the link between the agency and the periodical became conspicuously close: at that date Knight Frank and Rutley bought the firm of Walton and Lee, who had taken the first and only page of property advertising in the first issue of the paper and had secured an exclusive right to it. Thus in more ways than might be imagined Hudson, Riddell and Newnes were in the right place at the right time, and their new magazine was the product of its own era.

Chapter 2

ENTHUSIASMS AND OPPORTUNITIES

Edward Hudson had a passion for technical quality, and everything relating to *Country Life* had to be as good as he could make it, but that on its own would not have brought him success. Contemporary enthusiasms and opportunities in Victorian and Edwardian England have to be considered as well. It was an age of nostalgia and romantic patriotism, of yearning for the old ways of rural life and for the old manners of building, whether the naturalness of the vernacular or the Englishness of Tudorbethan. As David Watkin has explained in *The Rise of Architectural History*: 'By 1900 a new religion had been invented – or, at least, a new version of an old religion: the worship of England.' It was the age of Elgar as well as Lutyens.

It is not difficult to see how *Country Life* slotted into that mood, drawing inspiration from it as well as giving expression to it, and the picture can be filled out in various directions through recent writing. Martin J. Wieners's *English Culture and The Decline of The Industrial Spirit 1850-1980* makes the success of *Country Life* at times all too disturbingly intelligible. Raymond Williams's *The Country and The City* also throws light on it. Even more recently, in the catalogue to the 'British Art in the 20th Century' exhibition at the Royal Academy in 1987, there is a revealing essay by Robert Rosenblum on the 'Transatlantic View of British Painting'.

Martin Wiener writes of the development of the anti-industrial spirit in the late nineteenth century, the expansion of the middle class and its coming together with the old gentry and aristocracy partly through the public school, and the discovery 'that England was after all an old country, with a precious heritage in danger of obliteration. Concern grew to protect and reforge links with that heritage' and 'out of the midst of the new urban society "ruralism" rose up reborn.'

Raymond Williams has written: 'Rural Britain was subsidiary, and knew it was subsidiary, from the late nineteenth century. But so much of the past of the country, its feelings and its literature, was involved with rural experience, and so many ideas of how to live well, from the style of the country house to the simplicity of the cottage, persisted and even were strengthened, that there is almost an inverse proportion, in the twentieth century, between the relative importance of the working rural economy and the cultural importance of rural ideas.'

Robert Rosenblum's essay, of course, looks at the twentieth century from a different angle. He accepts the independence of British painting as part of its insularity: 'British twentieth-century art can seem so quirky and unpredictable that even some of its most famous imports to the United States after 1945 . . . seem thoroughly out of joint with main line art history, refusing to be computed by the categories that accommodate other artists. . . . One quickly discovers that Britain is a land in which all things forceful, intense and direct are clouded by veils of restraint and fluctuation. . . . Yet the view of British art in the twentieth century that would impose the evolutionary sequence of international Modernism or the standards of other countries needs constantly to be adjusted to take into account the stubborn facts of local experience and traditions.'

If that interpretation is applied to English architecture, its twentieth-century history becomes more intelligible, and the picture presented by *Country Life* in its years is seen to be closer to the historical perspective than seemed possible fifteen years ago.

The establishment of *Country Life* coincided with a period of optimism as far as domestic architecture was concerned. A considerable company of gifted architects and many well-endowed patrons, mainly middle-class as opposed to aristocratic, were becoming interested in the history of architecture, gardening and furniture. So it is convenient that in the year of *Country Life's* foundation, 1897, Reginald Blomfield brought out his two volume *History of Renaissance Architecture in England 1500-1800*: that gives a clear idea of current attitudes to periods, and, also, by starting with Authorities Consulted, it draws attention to the scantiness of architectural literature until the 1890s. Blomfield wrote in a curve of enthusiasm starting off in the days of Henry VIII , with architecture reaching 'its highest development in the hands of Inigo Jones and Wren, and eventually [running] itself out in the uncertainties induced by the literary eclecticism of the 18th century.' To him Wren was 'the greatest architect this country possessed, perhaps our one architect of quite commanding genius . . . the most English of all English architects', and the fifty years from the Restoration to the death of Queen Anne was the culminating point of modern English architecture. In contrast to that he found the work of the early eighteenth-century architects lacking 'in strong individuality . . . just a trifle cold and colourless.' For him neither Kent nor Adam were among the best architects of the eighteenth century. Moreover he ended on a note of gloom: the arts 'are not at present regarded as worthy of serious and sustained attention, and until some reasonable standard of judgement has grown into recognition among educated people it is not likely that there will be any general improvement in English architecture.'

The declining end to the curve, however, would not have found universal agreement: in 1904 Muthesius wrote of the smaller country houses: 'Not only do they represent the best in contemporary English architectural practice but they contain what is perhaps the best modern English art as a whole. If one thinks of all the branches of modern English art one comes to the conclusion that the best and most attractive work is to be found in the small country house.'

Three years before Blomfield's book came out J.A. Gotch published his two folio volumes on *The Architecture of the Renaissance in England*, a massive undertaking by Batsford consisting of fine photographs taken by Charles Latham and printed in collotype in Leipzig. As Gotch said, 'The art of fitly illustrating architecture by means of the camera has not been widely acquired and we hold ourselves fortunate in having secured the services of Latham.' Two years later Batsford published G.H. Birch's book on London churches, which must be the handsomest piece of preservation propaganda ever printed: it has 64 superb plates from finely conceived photographs by Charles Latham. In 1898 Batsford brought out a third important work, John Belcher and Mervyn Macartney's *Later Renaissance Architecture in England*. Alongside those books Blomfield's, which was published by Bell, is almost old fashioned in appearance, because, while he reproduced original architectural drawings and engravings and tipped in a few photographic illustrations, most of the plates are after his own appealing sketches in pen and ink.

The collotype plates in Gotch's and Birch's books must have been a revelation in the 1890s, but, as is explained in Hector Bolitho's *A Batsford Century* (1943), the process was slow and expensive, involving checking each copy of every plate with the printer for consistency of tone, and discarding a great many. So it could only be used for expensive books in comparatively small editions.

Here the development of half-tone printing on coated paper was crucial, because it introduced new possibilities of illustration not only for books but for periodicals too; but on its own it would not have brought about a revolution, and its introduction in the 1880s has to be related to improvements in photography taking place at the same moment. As Beaumont Newall wrote in *The History of Photography from 1839 to the Present Day*: 'Dry plates, flexible film, anastigmatic lenses [that allow for wider apertures and so shorter exposures at the same time as correcting distortions] and hand cameras made it possible to produce negatives more quickly, more easily, and of greater variety of subjects than ever before. The half-tone enabled these photographs to be reproduced economically and in limitless quantity in books, magazines and newspapers.' However it took some years for the process to be perfected, and although it was first used in a daily newspaper in New York in 1880, it was not used on speed presses until 1897.

Batsford, who had originally been booksellers and became publishers in 1874, seized on it for their expansion of their list of books on architecture and the decorative arts. Also a number of related illustrated magazines were started. *The Studio*, for instance, was founded in 1893: three years later The *Architectural Review* became an independent publication 'for the Artist, Archaeologist, Designer and Craftsman' as opposed to those concerned with the technical side of building. In 1901 *The Connoisseur* was started, and in 1903 *The Burlington Magazine*. And as competition increased, standards went up.

What is striking about the books and periodicals of that time is how much of the writing was by architects and craftsmen. In the field of books on historic architecture almost the first was J.A. Gotch's *The Buildings of Sir Thomas Tresham*, which Batsford published in 1883. Born in Kettering, in Northamptonshire, Gotch practised there and devoted much of his life to the study of architecture in the region, writing numerous books and articles, including some for *Country Life*, as well as carrying out many restorations.

Reginald Blomfield wrote with even more success, at least as far as his architectural career was concerned, starting out from articles on old Sussex ironwork in the mid 1880s and going on to books on gardens and then on to English and French architecture.

The names of most of the successful architects of the late nineteenth century and early twentieth century appear as contributors to *The Architectural Review*, but the most distinguished as a writer was undoubtedly A.E. Richardson, whose influential *Monumental Classic Architecture* was published in 1912. (Lutyens was unusual in writing little except for a handful of articles in *Country Life* and *The Architectural Review*.) Richardson's book is a splendid demonstration of how far taste and understanding of historic architecture had developed since Blomfield's book of 1897. Not only did he look at the classical achievement in the British Isles through fresh eyes, illustrating many unfamiliar Georgian buildings in Dublin, but he took the story down to 1880. Moreover he saw it as a pointer to the future: 'At the present time there is a growing appreciation for the academic phases of English Neo-Classic architecture; and more especially is attention being directed to the buildings conceived in the monumental manner.' Pointedly, however, he made no reference to Lutyens. It is surely an ironical coincidence that in that very year Lutyens was given the greatest classical opportunity ever presented to a British architect, to design the new imperial capital in Delhi.

In the field of craftsmanship, too, much of the writing was done by practitioners. Laurence Turner, whose *Decorative Plasterwork* was published by *Country Life* in 1927, was writing about the subject by 1905-06; and G.P. Bankart, the author of *The Art of the Plasterer* (1908), was the head of a business in Grays Inn Road.

By the late 1890s there was not only a rapidly growing interest in architecture and craftsmanship old and new, with greater opportunities to read about and look at illustrations of buildings, but there was an even more active interest in all aspects of gardens and gardening, with a comparable band of garden writers and growing possibilities of publication. Indeed it was a field particularly significant for *Country Life*, because it is arguable that it established its articles on gardens before its articles on houses, as will be explained.

Reginald Blomfield's first book, for instance, was on gardens rather than on historic architecture: *The Formal Garden in England*, a small book illustrated with fine drawings by Inigo Thomas, which appeared in 1892. In 1902 Batsford brought out H. Inigo Triggs' much more handsome *Formal Gardens in England and Scotland, Their Planning and Arrangement and Ornamental Features* illustrated with 72 plates of his drawings and 53 photographs by Charles Latham (and to which Lutyens subscribed).

In his preface Triggs wrote, 'It may perhaps be safely said that the revival which has taken place during the past decade is not only strong evidence of the continuing interest felt in the Art, but is also of great promise for the future, since it has attracted the attention of various classes, chief amongst which are amateurs of taste and means, together with architects who have made a special study of the Art as it was practised during the best periods of its history.'

One of the people he could have mentioned, but did not, was H. Avray Tipping, who wrote about gardens before he turned to houses in *Country Life*. And, of course, it was through gardens and writing about gardens that Edward Hudson first met Gertrude Jekyll. In 1900 he bought *The Garden*, the paper founded in 1871 by William Robinson which Gertrude Jekyll edited with E.T. Cook in 1900-01, and in 1901 he published her third and fourth gardening books.

Gertrude Jekyll was the best known woman gardener of her day, but she was by no means the only one who wrote, and her books were preceded by Alicia Amherst's *A History of Gardening*, which appeared in 1895. The third edition of this book published in 1910 (by which time the author had become Mrs Evelyn Cecil) includes an additional final chapter on Modern Gardening, which echoes the words of Inigo Triggs: 'Ten years before the close of the nineteenth century gardening was still the passion of the few, now it is the craze of the many. For every book on the subject that came out in 1895 a dozen appeared in 1905; for each person who then knew to what order a daisy belonged perhaps twenty could now be found, able to quote with ease five-syllabled Latin names.'

The enjoyment of old houses and of gardening went hand in hand with that of old furniture, but it took a little longer for that to develop a worthwhile literature of its own. Indeed throughout this century furniture history, as the subject had become, has followed in the wake of architectural history, and it is surely indicative of the situation that *The Connoisseur* should have started five years after *The Architectural Review*. There was already a liking for eighteenth-century furniture in the 1870s, about the same time as the fashion for eighteenth-century portraits; and by 1880, as can be seen at Haddo House in Aberdeenshire (fig. 5), where Wright and Mansfield worked for the 7th Earl of Aberdeen, some good decoration and fine furniture in a late eighteenth-century vein was being produced.

Perhaps the best short account of that revival is given by Muthesius, who related it to the taste of the aesthetic period: 'The delicate art of Chippendale and Sheraton was rediscovered at that time. The graceful little cabinets and little tables with spidery legs were brought out of store and were found to fit the present mood excellently.' And he continued, 'imitation eighteenth century furniture accounts for by far the largest part of present day demand. Sheraton reigns once more in the drawing room and bedroom, Chippendale chairs in the dining room.' That explains the first modern reprinting of Sheraton's and Hepplewhite's designs in 1895 and 1897.

5. *The morning room at Haddo House, Aberdeenshire, in 1966. Wright and Mansfield decoration of 1880*

Accurate knowledge, however, was shaky, and it was only in 1896 that Hungerford Pollen and Purdon Clarke put on the first exhibition of old English furniture and silks at the Bethnal Green Museum. It was considered that it 'would be of service to the two leading industries of the district, as well as instructive and interesting to the general public.' The memorandum circulated before the exhibition said: 'As recent changes of fashion have caused a demand for eighteenth century patterns of figured silk, which were formerly manufactured in the East of London, and as the designs of the early days of George III are now being revived or adapted, it will be of great advantage if the owners of dresses and costumes made of these silks will lend them for exhibition.'

Arguably the first useful history was that of Frederick Litchfield, who was a dealer: his *Illustrated History of Furniture* first appeared in 1892, but all its illustrations were based on drawings. The first major account illustrated with photographs was Percy Macquoid's *History of Furniture*, which appeared in four volumes between 1904 and 1908 (he became a contributor to *Country Life* in 1911). As H. Avray Tipping wrote in his introduction to Macquoid's and Edwards' great *Dictionary of English Furniture* published in 1924: 'Where anything approaching a complete treatment has been attempted there has been a measure of tentativeness and immaturity, arising from the obscurity that surrounded the subject until, some score of years ago, Mr Macquoid boldly undertook to dissipate the fog. His *History of Furniture* was the work of a pioneer . . . ' Tipping went on: 'Mr Macquoid was the first serious student to bestow time and attention on a comprehensive survey of the field, and to give to the public the results of his labours.'

How Percy Macquoid came to develop his interest and knowledge is a mystery. He was trained as a painter before working in the theatre. (Tipping, who wrote his obituary in *Country Life*, said: 'My friendship with him was of forty years' standing', and remembered 'his youthful studio when painting and illustration work were his leading interests.') David Beevers has suggested that it derived from his attempts at historical authenticity in his theatrical designs. In his entry in *Who's Who* Macquoid described himself as an artist, designer and decorator. In 1892 he married Theresa Dent, the daughter of a successful China merchant. They built The Yellow House in Bayswater, to the design of Ernest George and Peto, the latter being an old friend of Macquoid. Within a decade each room was devoted to a particular period of English or continental furniture and decorative art.

By 1900 there were a number of such collectors, among them Frank Green, who was restoring Treasurer's House at York (figs. 94, 95, 96), but they were having to feel their way forward without much help from the Victoria and Albert Museum. In 1908 Lady Dorothy Nevill lamented in her *Notebooks*: 'It is much to be deplored that the Victoria and Albert contains no throughly representative collection of old English furniture. True is it that a certain number of good examples are to be seen there, but these are more or less scattered about, no special section existing to show the evolution of style from Elizabethan times to the end of the eighteenth century. This is more to be regretted, as an assemblage of the best work of English cabinet makers such as Chippendale, Sheraton, Hepplewhite and others, could not fail to have an admirable educational effect upon public taste, especially were it displayed in rooms decorated in the style of the epoch.'

The growth of the Museum's collection of period rooms is in itself a comment on the history of taste. First in 1891 came the Sizergh Castle room and then in 1894 the room from the Old Palace at Bromley by Bow (fig. 6) which was widely copied by architectural decorators; they were followed in 1899 by Early Tudor Renaissance panelling from Green Yard at Waltham Abbey. It was only in 1903 that the Museum acquired its first eighteenth-century interior, from Cliffords Inn, and that was joined in 1910 and 1912 by the rooms from 5 Great George Street and Hatton Garden (fig. 7), the last partly through the support of *Country Life*. Both

6. *A period room at the Victoria and Albert Museum. The Bromley by Bow room as it was in 1914*

these rooms were shown stripped, which was to have a disastrous and longstanding influence on fashionable taste on both sides of the Atlantic.

If the Museum was slow to act, dealers saw the advantage of the right kind of background and began to buy fine old houses in which to show off their stock. Lenygon, at 31 Old Burlington Street from 1909, is now the best-known example, but there were others including Owen Grant, who occupied 11 and 12 Kensington Square. In 1909 they even commissioned H. Avray Tipping to write *A Short History of Kensington Square* that was really their brochure. In it he said 'the fine examples of furniture and decorative objects – so many of them contemporary with the building – which they place in the rooms, complete the picture of the past and make it a place of pilgrimage for those who desire to live again for a moment in the days of the last of the Stuarts and the first of the Hanoverians.'

Lenygon is particularly associated with the two books published in 1914 under the name of Francis Lenygon and called *Furniture in England 1660-1760* and *Decoration in England 1660-1770*. There was an F.H. Lenygon in the firm who concentrated on the American side of the business, but he had nothing to do with the writing of those books. Their genesis was explained in *The Batsford Centenary*. Early in 1914 Batsford, bought for £900 all the rights and hundreds of blocks from Colonel H.H. Mulliner 'who was a gun mounting fan, a furniture collector and Autolycus purchaser of all kinds of businesses' including Lenygons; and out of this material were produced not only those two books in 1914, but Margaret Jourdain's *The Early Renaissance* (1924) and *The Later Classical Revival* (1922) and W.G. Thomson's *Tapestry Weaving in England* (1914). The Lenygon books were the work of Colonel Mulliner and

*7. The Hatton Garden room at
the Victoria and Albert Museum
in 1915*

Margaret Jourdain, who had become a contributor to *Country Life* in 1906
and was also paid a retainer by Lenygons from 1911.

Of Colonel Mulliner, Philip Tilden wrote that he 'was the guiding
mind behind many enterprises, and if he groused at times because
cement or coach-building were not giving him the interest that he
had hoped, nevertheless he had cause for his grouses, for he devoted his wealth to matters of great cultural importance, to the firm of
Lenygon and Morant, and above all to his flat in the Albany.'

The interest in old textiles, tapestry and needlework was established
rather earlier. That had been encouraged not only by William Morris
and the growth of the collections at the Victoria and Albert Museum
but through such firms as Warners, Watts & Co and Morant. Benjamin
Warner (1828-1908) set up a small silk-weaving factory at Old Ford in
1870 and that was soon successful. In 1891 it became Warner and Sons,
and in 1895 it acquired Daniel Walters & Sons of Braintree. Watts &
Co had been started in 1868 by three architects, Bodley, Garner and the
younger Gilbert Scott, to provide needlework, textiles and wallpapers
that they and other architects could use on their jobs. Among those
who did was Temple Moore, who restored Treasurer's House (figs, 94,
95, 96) for Frank Green.

Morants, who joined up with Lenygons in 1915 and are usually
thought of in that connection, were well established long before that, and,
in addition to their normal work as upholsterers and decorators supplied
old materials or had them copied. At Dunham Massey in Cheshire, for
instance, there is still evidence of the kind of work that they did under
the direction of Percy Macquoid. They also restored the Holme Lacy bed
(fig. 110), having some of the damask specially rewoven.

The taste for old furniture and old materials encouraged the taste for old houses, for restoration and period fittings, and vice-versa. On the other hand period rooms, in the sense of everything in a room being of the same date, which the French and the Americans admire, have had little appeal in England since the late eighteenth century. The English enjoy a variety of allusion and generally feel more at home with pictures and objects of different dates and origins and in rooms that give a sense of continuity and natural development. Whatever the reasons for this attitude, it has had a profound influence on reactions to new houses and new architecture, both of which impose demands for a disciplined selectivity that few English people are prepared to accept. Curiously enough, this never seems to be discussed in connection with the Modern Movement and its history in England, probably because most writers about architecture are not interested in furniture and interiors.

The effect of the First World War in general was so profound that how it effected architecture seems a secondary consideration. At the simplest level it virtually destroyed the Edwardian social and economic world that had proved such a stimulating time for architects working in the domestic field, and it ended the demand for large new houses, if not for those of more modest size. That is particularly apparent in the practices of Edwin Lutyens, who built only two after 1918, and Detmar Blow, Robert Lorimer and John Kinross, who built none at all.

More fundamental, however, was the breach it created between architects practising before the War, many of whom had fought in it, and those who started to practise afterwards. Thus it encouraged a new climate of opinion in which architecture was seen to have new social as well as aesthetic priorities, with domestic architecture no longer being dominant. It also encouraged architects, if not clients, to start to think in international terms and to look abroad at what was happening in Holland and Sweden as well as France and – later – Germany.

At the same time, however, it had the opposite effect of strengthening the desire of those who were established to seek roots and a refuge in history and tradition and, as economic pressure and planning threats were seen to be inexorably increasing, to discover the point of preservation in many different forms. Money was still reasonably plentiful in the 1920s and, although households were employing fewer servants, machinery was becoming more useful and there was no loss of enthusiasm for old houses and their restoration. So that remained a very active field throughout the inter-war years. Indeed it should not be discounted in any architectural history of the period, because it explains a great deal about what did not happen. Again, it was not just an architectural interest, but related to publishing and to enthusiasms for antique furniture and for gardening.

The enthusiasm for old houses seems to divide very roughly into an earlier one for mediaeval and Tudor to Jacobean houses and a later one for classical houses of the late seventeenth to the early nineteenth century. Of course that was not a hard and fast divide, but it is striking what a strong sense of chronological development there was in the pages of *Country Life*. During the 1920s there was a revival of the pre-war enthusiasm

for restoring castles and manor houses: work was resumed at Allington Castle, Herstmonceaux (figs. 148, 149, 150), Saltwood and St Donat's, and an elaborate internal remodelling was started at Leeds Castle. Country house restoration was still a possible pleasure, as can be seen at Dartington in Devon and Parham in Sussex (figs. 10, 65) and in many smaller manor houses like Cold Ashton (figs. 190, 191), and Westwood (figs. 197, 198). And if for some reason it was not possible to move, a successful manor house could be recreated, as was done by the Messels at Nymans in Sussex (figs. 8, 233, 234).

It was difficult, however, to have Romance without Draughts, and during the 1920s people became increasingly aware of American ideas of plumbing and heating. And as dress became less formal and structured, oak settles and high backed chairs of the kind favoured by people like the Messels, began to seem too stiff, Nymans was not comfortable in the modern sense; nor were houses like Cold Ashton and Westwood, where owners were not prepared to sacrifice atmosphere and appearance to convenience.

At the same time there was a growing enthusiasm for the eighteenth century: for its architecture, its furniture and decoration and for certain aspects of its painting. So while in 1921 the Royal Commission on Historical Monuments cautiously extended its brief from 1700 to 1714, more people were moving further into the century, preparing to go beyond Queen Anne to Vanbrugh and Adam and even to Soane and the Regency. Among the most interesting projects tackled in the period were the Ronald Trees' refurnishing and redecoration of first Kelmarsh (fig. 11) and then Ditchley, Philip Sassoon's remodelling of Trent (figs. 225, 226, 227), the Ionides's redecoration and refurnishing of Buxted (figs. 224, 225), and

8. *Nymans, Sussex. A romantic manor house formed in the 1920s round an existing undistinguished house*

28

9. *Allington Castle, Kent. A restoration begun before and completed after the First World War*

the Trittons' alteration of Godmersham (fig. 12). Remarkably little of this phase, however, survives today. Perhaps the best example is Plas Newydd in North Wales, remodelled by the same Lord Anglesey who had earlier carried out an Old English transformation of Beaudesert (figs. 164, 165).

These were the exceptional houses of the time, but many smaller houses were restored and redecorated, as is apparent from the many articles in *Country Life* under the headings 'Country Homes' and 'Lesser Country Houses'. A number of books reflected this development, among them Stanley C. Ramsay and J.D.M. Harvey's *Small Houses of the Late Georgian Period 1750-1820* (Vol.1, 1919, on exteriors, and Vol.2, 1923, on interiors and details); Margaret Jourdain's *English Interiors From Smaller Houses of the Seventeenth to the Nineteenth Century* (1923); and Richardson and Eberlin's *The Smaller English House of the Later Renaissance 1660-1830* (1925).

Rather surprisingly there was less serious interest in most aspects of English painting, perhaps a reaction against the taste of the Duveen generation for grand portraits. Instead there was a slow growth of interest in conversation pictures that was particularly associated with Sir Philip Sassoon. This taste for what is essentially undemanding went with a liking for simpler and lighter decoration and furnishing.

Although the attitudes and enthusiasms of potential patrons, such as those who owned the houses mentioned here and illustrated later, have been generally ignored in the history of twentieth-century architecture, they do much to explain the slow development of enthusiasm for new architecture between the Wars, the eventual victory of the Modern Movement after the Second World War (when private employment of architects all but

29

12. Tea in the Garden, Godmersham *by Rex Whistler. A conversation piece showing Mr and Mrs Robert Tritton with the new south front designed for them about 1935 by Walter Sarell*

10. (Opposite left) *The great hall at Parham Park, Sussex in 1951. Its rearrangement by Mr and Mrs Clive Pearson in the years after 1922 can be compared with its appearance in 1902 in Fig 65*

11. (Opposite right) *The entrance hall at Kelmarsh Hall, Northamptonshire, in 1933. It had been recently redecorated by Mr and Mrs Ronald Tree*

ceased,) and the way the supporters of the Movement dominated writing about architecture until the mid 1970s.

So far no one has written with sympathy about the traditional strand, whether its roots lay in the Arts and Crafts movement or in classicism, and the Modern Movement, and the relationship between taste in architecture and other aspects of the applied and decorative arts. Indeed, few people would dare now to tackle Lutyens and Le Corbusier and see the strengths and weaknesses of both.

With characteristic wisdom and perception John Summerson wrote an introduction to Trevor Dannatt's *Modern Architecture in Britain* (1959) in which he said: 'It seems natural, writing about the past thirty years of English architecture, to write as if the only things worth bothering about were the local initiation, progress and achievements of the "modern movement". Historically, this is evidently lop-sided; but also historically, it would be extremely difficult to write about the architecture of the period as if it could all be evaluated in much the same way. It cannot be. In architecture, as in painting and sculpture, there has been a deep and wide gulf between the moderns and those who are vaguely and rather misleadingly described as traditionalists.'

And he continued: 'It has always seemed to me that 1927 was the crucial year for England, the year in which scattered and indiscriminate observation of events on the continent coalesced into an opinion – that such a thing as a "modern movement" existed and was in the nature of a "cause".

'For about six years after 1927, it must be admitted, the modern movement in England was mostly talk: talk, travel and illustration. Nothing of substantial importance in the new spirit was built here before 1933. Meanwhile there was the great slump of 1929-1932 which hit the architectural profession especially hard. Adversity (in a measure), not prosperity, makes people turn to new things and it was in the depressed years that the modern idea caught on.'

Here no attempt can be made to provide an outline history of the period 1918-1935, but I hope that both what is said about the approach of *Country Life* in those years, and the selection of illustrations, will give an impression of how the period seemed to those running the magazine and particularly to Christopher Hussey. To depict *Country Life* as a pillar of reaction is too simple – a distortion of Christopher Hussey's approach, particularly in the 1920s and 1930s: he was deeply concerned with the right progress of architecture and planning while underlining the value of the English and Scottish traditions in the face of what seemed an increasingly alien and insensitive internationalism. In order to understand his aims, however, it is necessary to see how the English reaction to the Modern Movement related to them.

The key events were the publication of Le Corbusier's *Vers une architecture* in 1923 and the staging of *L'Exposition des Arts Decoratifs et Industriels Modernes* in Paris in 1925. Basil Ward later wrote of Le Corbusier's Pavillon there: 'It stood out in all its purity and strength of expression in a post-war rag bag of resurrected "Movements" and "styles".

But the Art Deco style was far more easily assimilated and it became a substitute for modern architecture, an easy tool for those architects (and there were many in England) who regarded the Modern Movement as only a stylistic revolution.'

Among younger architects who went to the exhibition was Amyas Connell (1901-1980), a New Zealander, who made the journey to Paris on his way to England. He then went as a prize winner to the British School in Rome, where the Director was Professor Bernard Ashmole; and it was Ashmole who gave him the commission to design High and Over (figs. 13, 222, 223, 234).

The new movement had a natural appeal to that younger generation, and here it is useful to have the memories of one of the most influential writers on architecture, J.M. Richards, in *Memoirs of An Unjust Fella*. He was a student at the Architectural Association from 1924 to 1929 when 'the school was still dominated by the traditional teaching methods of the many schools of architecture modelled on the Ecole des Beaux Arts in Paris. . . . A few, including Howard Robertson, the Principal, did know something of the changes taking place in Europe, but these hardly influenced the AA curriculum. . . . We read the magazines and the latest books (the first English version of Le Corbusier's *Vers une architecture* came out in 1927, when I was in my third year) and even if there were not many revolutionary new buildings to look at at home, we knew enough to plan itineraries of our vacation tours on the Continent to take in pioneer modern buildings.' J.M. Richards joined *The Architectural Journal* in July, 1933.

Two other magazines serving architectural interests were *The Architect and Building News* and *The Architectural Review*. The exhibition of the architectural photographs of F.R. Yerbury at the Architectural Association in March, 1986, together with the accompanying book by Andrew Higgot, was an excellent reminder of his influence. Although he was not trained as a photographer, he had an excellent eye for architecture, and his role was important in making new work in Holland, Sweden and Germany, as well as France, familiar in England. Altogether between 1920 and 1930 he illustrated 150 articles written by Howard Robertson, the American Principal of the AA, with whom he regularly travelled.

Comparison between *Country Life* and *The Architectural Review* is particularly instructive in the 1920s. The element of parallelism is much greater, and the *Review's* progressiveness less consistent, than might be expected. To take *Country Life* first, in the first half of 1924, there were articles on Lutyens' Doll's House (figs. 44, 181-86), on two town house interiors by Oliver Hill, on eighteenth-century decoration at Saltram by Margaret Jourdain, and – surely most surprising – no less than seven pages on the Tudor House addition to Liberty's. In the second half of 1924 came the last of four articles on modern German architecture, on Walter Gropius. In the review of the Paris exhibition in 1925 there was no picture of Le Corbusier's Pavillon. In the first half of the following year Christopher Hussey contributed an article on Vanbrugh to mark the bicentenary of his death; in the second half of the year a fake half-timbered house overlooking the golf course at Sandwich was published and so was

13. *High and Over,
Buckinghamshire, designed by
Amyas Connell in 1929–31*

New Ways at Northampton, the first modern house ever built in England, with a photograph to show how un-neighbourly it was, the caption saying 'An amusing photograph which emphasizes the tremendous clash of contrast between the two types of houses.'

Of course, it has to be remembered that editorial policy is never completely free, and the interests of the editor and contributors have to be balanced with those of readers and advertisers; also it is dependent on the material available, which may not be as up to the minute as the contributors would like.

In the case of *The Architectural Review* the key was provided by the increasing influence of Hubert de Cronin Hastings, the son of Percy Hastings, who had been involved with the paper since 1899. H. de C. Hastings had been to the Slade, then run by Tonks, where he came on Cezanne and Cubism, and then went on to the Bartlett School of Architecture (as Susan Lasdun explained in *Harpers & Queen* for April, 1985). He began full time work at the *Review* in 1922. Three years later he became interested in the Modern Movement, but it was only after two or three more years, when he became Editor, that modern subjects became dominant and the design and layout of the magazine and the style of photography were replanned to suit them.

The problem of the continuity of tradition and coming to terms with new developments in architecture is particularly well illustrated in the career of Oliver Hill. Born in 1887, he started to practise in 1910. His career was brought to an abrupt halt by the First World War, during which he served in the London Scottish Regiment and was awarded the Military Cross. Afterwards he had to start again from scratch, developing what became a very successful practice. Perhaps more than any other architect he holds a key to understanding the period from 1928 to 1940. David Dean, in *The Thirties: Recalling the English Architectural Scene*, wrote of him as 'a man who slipped in and out of modernism . . . Romantic, enthusiastic to the point of extravagance and sometimes beyond, he moved easily from style to style: Tudor, Georgian, Lutyensesque, Pseudism, even Provençal and not least a Moderne-inflected modernism. But he was more than literally style-ish, there was an aplomb, a dashing elegance running through all his work.'

I got to know him only in the late 1960s, when he was in his late seventies, living at Daneway in Gloucestershire, an early Cotswold house which he had handled with great imagination as well as boldness. He loved seventeenth- and early eighteenth-century oak and walnut furniture, tapestry and old glass, and he combined the sophisticated with the simple and rustic. Also there were relics of his enthusiasm for what had been new in the 1920s and 30s, in particular textiles. The place was not only the home of an architect with a marvellous eye and a wide range of visual and historical enthusiasms; it also explained how he had been able to work in such a variety of styles, and it explained his remark quoted by David Dean, 'Grace, it seems to me, is the supreme desirability in fine architecture.'

From the *Country Life* point of view Oliver Hill is an interesting figure, because, as is explained later, he is one of the architects who recognised his debt to the magazine and became closely associated with it. He had first discovered it while at school at Uppingham, and through it was introduced both to old houses and to the work of Lutyens. After he left school, he went to see Lutyens, a life-long hero, who recommended that he should start by working in a builder's yard for eighteen months. That experience heightened his pleasure in the texture of building materials. Then from 1907 to 1910 he trained in the office of William Flockhart, which Margaret Richardson has described as the most artistic of the period, and not only did that probably encourage his eclectic approach, but it developed his talent as a draughtsman and watercolourist, which related to his fundamentally painterly approach to architecture: he was never much concerned with intellectual or social theories. That too was to be important in his approach to the Modern Movement, and what Modern Movement figures thought about him: they did not believe that he was serious.

Perhaps the most revealing impression of him is that given by Charles Reilly in his autobiography written in 1938: he knew him well, enjoying his company and admiring his work. 'Hill can build and furnish a better modern house, free from all stylistic reflections, than anyone else,' he wrote, 'and that is what he really likes doing. His knowledge of other ways of expression really bears out my contention that no one can be successfully "modern" who does not know, and know well, the old ways too . . . He is the Augustus John of architecture who can do everything superbly well and who has now done everything up to a point but has not yet painted his great School of Athens, that is has not yet built his great composition.'

In this he was the victim of his time, because just as the First World War delayed the start of his career, the Second World War cut off his period of maturity. Certainly he felt that. However, between the Wars he had a very successful practice as can be seen from the numerous articles on his buildings, many of them in *Country Life*.

The architectural situation in the late 1920s and early 1930s, already bedevilled by the battle between two fundamentally different approaches that was developing, was further complicated by new subjects of concern: planning and preservation, the spoliation of the landscape, the destruction of historic buildings in towns and the increasing threats to country houses. In the field of the preservation of landscape, Clough Williams Ellis played an influential role. Portmeirion, his fantasy on the coast of North Wales, was first conceived as a serious demonstration about placing buildings in landscape. He wrote a great deal about threats to the landscape, most notably in *England and the Octopus* (1928), and he also took practical steps, such as acquiring stretches of landscape in North Wales for preservation, and saving the Grand Avenue at Stowe in 1923.

In London the great private houses that had been described by Beresford Chancellor in his *Private Palaces of London* (1908) continued to be demolished: Devonshire House, most of Lansdowne House, Grosvenor House, Norfolk House, Kingston House, Dorchester House. A new degree of concern was apparent in the unsuccessful attempts to save Dorchester House (figs. 206, 207); while the Crown Estate's proposal in 1932 to demolish Carlton House Terrace and replace it with a new scheme designed by Reginald Blomfield, stirred up not only critics of new building but defenders of old (although until John Summerson wrote his book on *John Nash* in 1935, Nash was not really on the map of major architects). A key figure who was converted to the cause of classical architecture at about this time was Robert Byron, whose earlier interests had been in Middle Eastern architecture and art. In 1931 he had been commissioned by both *The Architectural Review* and *Country Life* to write articles to mark the completion of Lutyens' Delhi and the Viceroy's House, and it was he who became the most forceful figure in the foundation of the Georgian Group in 1937.

The new-found enthusiasm for the eighteenth century brought with it a growing interest in country houses and awareness of the threats to them, but at that stage there was little that could be done about it, given the Government's refusal to consider tax relief. The National Trust in the late 1920s was still a small and impecunious society. In 1932, when the question of its chairmanship came up, R.C. Norman refused to take it on, because, foreseeing the time when the Trust could be asked to take on great houses and great estates, he felt that it ought to be held by a landowner. Two years later Lord Lothian made what became a famous speech at the National Trust's annual meeting that led to the formulation of the Country Houses scheme.

That concern was spreading is apparent from the birthday message that Lord Onslow sent to *Country Life* on May 18, 1935: ' . . . It has among other services rendered one in particular, namely, the description in minute detail of all the great Country Houses of England as they were actually lived in as the houses of their owners. Perhaps in twenty years' time none will exist in that condition . . . '

To sum up, in the early half of the 1930s attitudes towards architectural style were confused. On the one hand, historical appreciation was expanding to take in the Regency period, with one progressive element seeing a parallel between the architecture of the Regency and a modern simplified classicism, and there was a growing awareness of landscape design and concern for the preservation of landscape, accompanied by increasing anxiety at the destruction of historic buildings both in towns and the country. On the other hand there was a new view of architecture which saw it as having new purposes and demanding new techniques. In addition there were political and social interpretations of architecture and of art in general which had their sources in the different kinds of totalitarianism developing in Russia, Germany and Italy. From the point of view of an architectural magazine such as *The Architectural Review* the issues involved may have seemed divisive, but they did at least involve only one discipline. For *Country Life* the situation was far more complex, because it had developed its interests in so many directions, and these divergent interests acted upon each other in a variety of ways.

Chapter 3

PEOPLE AND PLACES

'The history of a house is also the history of a culture, and the modern English house engages our attention largely because of the high level of culture it expresses. But only in history can we trace the steps by which the domestic culture that is so highly evolved today has developed.' Muthesius.

In 1898 *Country Life* introduced a decorative headpiece (fig. 3) for its articles on houses designed by J. Byam Shaw, and the series was given the title Country Homes and Gardens Old and New. That title deserves consideration, because 'Country Homes' is not the same as 'Country Houses', and that in itself says a good deal about the way attitudes have changed over the past ninety years. Today most people think of *Country Life's* regular articles as being about 'country houses', words which suggest associations with land and history as well as architecture; whereas 'country homes' sounds essentially liveable, and does not necessarily imply a surrounding estate or any historical interest. From 1898 Edward Hudson obviously envisaged the broader perspective, with the possibility of articles about new houses and gardens as well as old; and, indeed, experimental attempts were made to start various series of articles on smaller new houses: *New Homes in Old Houses, Village Houses for Holiday Homes* and *Houses for People with Hobbies*. Occasionally, also, there were articles on chateaux in France and palaces and villas in Italy.

The interest in smaller houses fitted in with Hudson's attitude to his own life. Soon after starting the magazine he met Gertrude Jekyll, and she introduced him to Edwin Lutyens; and by the autumn of 1899 Hudson had commissioned Lutyens to design a house. The idea of making a garden and of building a house must already have been in his mind, and his feeling as to which was the more important is expressed by its original name: The Deanery Garden, at Sonning (figs. 14, 17, 72, 73).

Edward Hudson is a rather baffling figure. Ralph Edwards, who could never have been described as easy and who got to know him in the office in the early 1920s, at the end of his own life wrote 'He was the very image of a British bourgeois, a typical minor establishment figure.' That is suspiciously close to Lytton Strachey's description in 1918 quoted on page 339 of Volume II of Michael Holroyd's *Life* (1968): 'A pathetically dreary figure. . . . A kind of bourgeois gentilhomme.' Yet to

14. (Opposite above) *The courtyard at The Deanery Garden, Sonning, Berkshire. This was the first house designed for Edward Hudson by Edwin Lutyens in 1899*

15 and 16. (Opposite below) *Edward Hudson in middle and later life.*

17. (Above) *The garden front of The Deanery Garden*

Major A.C.J. Congreve, who as a small boy used to go with his mother and his two elder brothers to Edward Hudson's house in Queen Anne's Gate and to stay at Lindisfarne Castle (figs. 19, 133, 134, 135) on the Northumberland coast, he was a much loved figure, kind to all of them. He was particularly devoted to Lady Congreve, even asking her to marry him in the mid 1930s, and he had intended to leave Lindisfarne to her eldest son, Billy, who was killed in 1917. Major Congreve remembers that soon after he married in 1928, Edward Hudson gave a soirée for him and his wife, asking Suggia, who was his other great love, and Segovia to play for them. And in 1967 it was Pamela Maude, who married Billy Congreve three weeks before he was killed, who wrote a touching memoir about Hudson in *Country Life*.

Hudson and Lady Emily Lutyens did not get on, but that is no reflection on him. However he was always kind to the Lutyens children, as Mary Lutyens recalled in *Edwin Lutyens* (1980): 'Hudson was a tall man, very kind, but unattractively plain. He was Ursula's godfather and often came to our nursery. . . . He was very good natured. We had a fire-screen in the nursery, the bottom part of which could be moved up leaving a gap at the bottom. It was perfect for playing French Revolutions, and Hudson was most obliging in kneeling on the floor and putting his head through the gap so that we could guillotine him. At Christmas time, when Father was in India, it would embarrass Mother dreadfully when

18. (Opposite above) *Tabley Old Hall, Cheshire in 1923. Hudson corrected photographs like this as if they were a watercolour. On the back of the original print are instructions to the printer:* 'Tone down water a little *and lighten cows a little*'

19. (Opposite below) *Lindisfarne Castle, Northumberland. Lutyens recreated the castle for Edward Hudson in 1903*

20. (Above) *A 17th-century Dutch painting re-interpreted. Barbara Lutyens photographed while staying at Lindisfarne in 1906*

he took her with all of us to Liberty's toy department, then the most expensive in London, to choose presents without giving her any idea of how much he wanted to spend.'

Lutyens, of course, was a very close friend of Hudson's, and, as Christopher Hussey wrote, 'both had much in common in their natures. Both were largely self-educated, with an instinctive appreciation of beauty; both were inarticulate . . . '

Although Hudson is not known to have ever written a word in *Country Life*, he was more personally involved with many of the details of the articles about houses and furniture than any subsequent editor, apart from Christopher Hussey. Quite often he visited houses to decide whether they should be included in the series and also to make the photographic notes, sometimes going with Avray Tipping, as later he was to do with Christopher Hussey. That is apparent in an early letter to the latter: 'I should just make notes & plans of Rooms showing what you propose to Photo – keep them in Books – . . . I make plans of the Rooms for house or Garden. With arrows showing what I want photographed. Some of the arrow points I mark a b c d etc. I also note the furniture about the House & suggest moving it – to various rooms if necessary & also I note what they are *not* to bring into a picture.' The little note books he mentioned were specially made up out of squared paper and they were given to the photographers when they went to do a job. Hudson also checked the quality of all the prints from the negatives, and on a few of the old prints still in use are his corrections or instructions to the printer, which suggest a sensitive eye influenced by watercolour painting.

Sadly and rather oddly, the only group – or rather fragments – of his letters that I have come across are to Margaret Jourdain, who used to write her notes, now in the Victoria and Albert Museum, on any scrap of paper that came to hand. Thus there are quite a lot of half letters from him written in the 1920s: they are markedly businesslike and impersonal considering that writer and recipient had known each other since 1906, but they show how closely he was concerned with every aspect of what she published in the magazine, going to see what was for sale and occasionally taking her with him.

One fragment, dated November 23, 1927, is revealing for the light it throws on his practicality as a businessman: 'I think you give too much notice to people like Rice & Christy and to Connell. We never seem to be able to get these people to advertise with us. Can you give us any assistance here? Of course, if they will not advertise, we must pay more attention to people who will.'

Hudson, of course, took a special interest in seeing that Lutyens' buildings, and after the First War not just his domestic work, were illustrated at the first good opportunity, and, starting with the first rather tentative article on Crooksbury (fig. 21), published on September 15, 1900, there are a steady stream.

Lutyens' success seems so assured that it is interesting to see how he struck Muthesius in 1904. 'He is a young man who of recent years

21. *Crooksbury, Surrey. The 1898 addition. The first house by Lutyens to be illustrated in* Country Life *in 1900*

22. *The* Country Life *building
in Tavistock Street, Covent
Garden designed by Lutyens in
1904*

has come increasingly to the forefront of domestic architecture and who
may soon become the accepted leader among English builders of houses,
like Norman Shaw in the past. Lutyens is one of those architects who
would refuse to have anything whatever to do with any new movement.
His buildings reflect his attachment to the styles of the past, the charms
of which he finds inexhaustible. . . . but just as a really important artist
cannot ignore the demands of his time, so Lutyens' new buildings do not
really look ancient at all. On the contrary, they have a character that if
not modern, is entirely personal and extremely interesting. . . . He is less
interested in making the interior a work of art. He is content with the
extreme simplicity of the country cottage or where luxury is called for,
imitation of an earlier style.'

Hudson's own taste, or his acceptance of Lutyens' development, also
deserves comment, because it was not only significant for *Country Life*,
but it illustrates so graphically changing attitudes in the late 1890s and
early 1900s. Without attempting a potted history of domestic architecture
in the first fourteen years of the century, of which Roderick Gradige has
given an account in *Dream Houses* (1980) and which Clive Aslet has
described in a broader context in *The Last Country Houses* (1982), it is
worth bearing in mind the change of mood from the vernacular style of

23. *The entrance hall of the* Country Life *building*

The Deanery Garden (fig. 17) of 1899 to the almost abstract treatment of Lindifarne Castle (fig. 19) in 1903 and then to the full Wrenaissance of the *Country Life* building in Tavistock Street designed in 1904.

Lutyens' office was a stimulating background for seventy-two years and its loss undermined the editorial staff's sense of identification with the magazine. In many ways it was impractical, but it gave pleasure every day. From the outset it was intended to look like a slice of Hampton Court Palace, and the main editorial offices were on the *piano nobile*. Care was taken with the handling of the entrance hall to create a dignified architectural effect, but the staircase always felt like a secondary stair in a country house, because there was insufficient space for it.

Then, however, there was a sense of arrival on the *piano nobile*, which was actually the second floor, because of a low mezzanine between it and the ground floor. Here there were five double height rooms looking north over the Market, and originally all five could be opened up. The detail was simple but bold, so that the rooms felt like those in a country house of about 1700, and the Editor's room (figs. 24, 25) was particularly

24. and 25. *The Editor's Room*
as it was in 1973

26. *Composing Room at Country Life. It was in the big roof space*

handsome, because, as well as having an overmantel painted with a still life it retained a good eighteenth-century glazed bookcase and other pieces of furniture that had belonged to Edward Hudson.

The imposing elevation (fig. 22), with its big roof designed to take the composing room (fig. 26), and tall chimneystacks (later the wall above the main cornice was pierced by white painted windows to light an extra storey of offices), and the suite of five rooms, disguised the shallowness of the site; everything was sacrificed to appearances, and at the back there were poky offices looking out onto dark internal light wells. It is typical that Dorothy Stroud, who worked at *Country Life* before the Second World War, remembers the difficulty of getting at the bound volumes of *Country Life*, which could only be housed in the men's lavatory.

It is surely remarkable that one patron should commission not only the last and finest of an architect's early works but should also follow that up with two firsts in quite different veins. Hudson possessed those indefinable qualities of an inspiring patron that enable an artist to give of his best. Moreover that was also to be part of the secret of his success as Editor of *Country Life*: he was able to get the best out of a remarkable company of contributors who remained loyal for many years. That is all the more remarkable, because he lacked grace and charm in his dealings with colleagues and was tempted to bully those whom he thought he could.

In fact the office does not seem to have been a particularly happy place, as emerges in letters from Bernard Darwin to Christopher Hussey. The first, dated February 15, 1939, was to thank him for a sympathetic letter: 'I did my best at a job which knowing the minds, if I may so term them, of the directors – I always felt must fail in the end. But in the adapted words of Mr Buzfuzz, "As to the Board I will say little; the subject presents but few attractions." I thank you very much indeed for what you say.' The second, dated November 2, 1940, about Christopher Hussey's giving up the Editorship, says 'I have now been at CL for roughly two & thirty years and it has been a d-d restless place all the time.'

Having got the magazine off the ground in 1897 and seen that it was likely to become established, it was natural that Hudson should have looked at contemporary publishing on architecture and gardening and realised that *Country Life* was in a unique position to produce handsomely illustrated books that made commercial sense. The material and, even more important, the photographs were flowing in all the time, and it was not too great a labour to re-use them in book form. Thus what started out, no doubt, as a simple commercial idea was to prove enormously stimulating to *Country Life* until 1970, when the old Book Department at the top of the Tavistock Street building was removed and completely separated from the magazine. While many of the architectural and gardening books were based on existing material, they also stimulated the authors to write articles so that both the texts and photographs existed for the books that they planned. It was an entirely practical arrangement that, alas, exists no longer.

How early it started is not clear, but, while it may not have applied in the volumes of *Gardens Old and New* or *English Homes*, it is likely that it influenced Tipping's plans for his fourth volume of the latter, published in 1912; and it was certainly happening in 1913 when Arthur Bolton began his series of articles on Adam buildings. Conceivably Lawrence Weaver's role was the crucial one, because as well as being Architectural Editor from 1909 he was the general editor of *The Architects Library*, the subtitle chosen for the series of *Country Life* folio books starting with his book on Lutyens.

Edward Hudson had an eye for old furniture as well as for houses and gardens, and his London house, 15 Queen Anne's Gate (fig. 27), contained some good pieces that he left to the Victoria and Albert Museum. So given his interest and the title of Charles Latham's *In English Homes*, it is not surprising to find articles on furniture in the early years. The first seems to have been on September 5, 1903 on a group of seventeenth-century chairs at Levens Hall, and that was followed on January 23, 1904 and March 12, 1904 by articles on armchairs and chests of drawers and cabinets; and two years later R. Freeman-Smith wrote the first article on eighteenth-century English furniture. But, as with the articles on houses, it took time to find the right contributors, and it was only in 1906 that *Country Life* published its first article by Margaret Jourdain.

Miss Jourdain is another of the all too misty figures in the early history of *Country Life*. Although she wrote many articles and books over

27. *Edward Hudson's Drawing Room at 15 Queen Anne's Gate. The chimneypieces look as if they were designed by Lutyens*

a period of almost fifty years, she never attempted anything personal or autobiographical, and, as Hilary Spurling found when writing *Ivy When Young* and *Secrets of a Woman's Heart*, her life of I. Compton Burnett, there are only scraps of information about Margaret Jourdain's life before she began to share Ivy Compton Burnett's flat in 1919. She was eighth out of ten children of the Rev. Francis Jourdain, Vicar of Ashbourne, most of whom were talented, original people able to overcome the material difficulties that faced the family. After getting a third at Oxford in 1897, she lived with her widowed mother in Dorset and published her first work in 1902, a revision of Mrs Palliser's *History of Lace* written in collaboration with Alice Dryden, who was ten years older. Alice Dryden was the only daughter of Sir Henry Dryden of Canons Ashby (figs. 173, 174, 175), a well known antiquarian of his day who encouraged the study of his ancient house, and it may have been at Canons Ashby in the 1890s that Margaret Jourdain started to develop her eye for the decorative arts. In 1903 she and Alice Dryden collaborated on *Memorials of Old Northamptonshire*, and thereafter she turned her hand to a broad range of subjects, including furniture, in order to make a modest living, increasing her output from three articles that year to sixty in 1911. In 1909 she was joined at *Country Life* by Percy Macquoid, an old friend of Tipping who had recently established his reputation with his four folio volume *History of English Furniture*. They were published between 1904 and 1908 by Lawrence and Bullen and contained a number of colour plates.

The latter evidently impressed Hudson. In April 1911, *Country Life* announced: ' . . . so great is the present interest in the history of furniture' that the magazine 'will week by week present a picture of a piece of furniture so exactly catching its characteristics . . . that the very thing will appear to stand before us.' The first piece honoured by the new process was a William and Mary needlework settee.

One of the imbalances, indeed injustices, of *Country Life* is that while authors on the staff have had their names at the top of country house articles since 1942, the staff photographers only started to receive acknowledgement at the end of the articles in 1970. As a result of this far too little is known about them. That is particularly unfortunate in the case of Charles Latham, who, as the founder of the *Country Life* tradition of architectural photography, had an extraordinarily wide influence on the way people in England were to look at buildings. He seems to have first worked for the paper about 1898, but he was already a recognised specialist in his field, because he took the plates for Gotch's *The Architecture of the Renaissance in England*, where he is described as 'of Balham'. Happily, he is remembered in *A Batsford Century*, where Harry Batsford recalled: 'The mention of [Thomas] Harris's name reminds me of his skirmish with Charles Latham, the lame photographer, also one of the friends of the shop, whom he called, rather unkindly, "Dot and Carry One". Latham was a brilliant photographer, and took many of the photographs of City churches, country houses and gardens for *Country Life* and for us. His talent went with a red beard and an entire absence of the letter H. Once he went to take photographs of a fine house which had been ruined inside by Victorian meddling. Latham hobbled into the room, stared round and said to the owner, "'ateful and 'ideous. I'm glad I kept my cab." Then he stumped out.'

Latham had taken the photographs for G.H. Birch's *London City Churches* published by Batsford in 1896. 'All the plates were photographed specially by Charles Latham on 15 x 12 plates at £3 10s an exposure, plus heavy expenses. The enlargement now increasingly employed was anathema. For some of the City church interiors Latham gave, with the slow plates of the day, twenty-four-hour exposure. The ghosts of stray people who sat down and went away may be seen on the plates.'

There are occasional mentions of Latham's name in articles in *Country Life*, but full recognition came in the handsome folios of *Gardens Old and New* followed by *In English Homes* where his name is more prominent than the editor's, the text being revisions of articles from the magazine done to support his splendid photographs. It is not known when he died or retired, but probably there is a clue in that the third volume of *In English Homes* published in 1909 was the last of the series.

Another much better-known architectural photographer employed by *Country Life* was Frederick Evans (1852-1943), who was commissioned to photograph French chateaux in 1905. Quite how long that assignment lasted is not clear, but the articles continued to be published throughout the First World War, only finally being gathered together in *Twenty-Five Great Houses of France* by Sir Theodore Andrea Cook (1917).

Good writers about country houses were as much a problem as good photographers in the early days. The first was John Leyland, who was primarily interested in naval, international and historical subjects, and as well as contributing to *The Times*, *The Daily Chronicle* and *The Observer*, was editor of the *Army and Navy Gazette* from 1904-1909. He had also written two books that might seem more relevant to *Country Life*, on *The Peak of Derbyshire* in 1891 and *The Yorkshire Coast* in 1892. Perhaps he met Hudson through *Navy and Army Illustrated*, one of the papers that Hudson and Newnes owned. He never developed any special knowledge of houses or gardens, although he edited the first volume of Charles Latham's *Gardens Old and New*. He seems to have given up after that.

Another early writer about houses was C.J. Cornish, a classical master at St Paul's School. According to *Who was Who*, he wrote for *The Spectator*, mainly on natural history, sport and out-door subjects. There is no mention of *Country Life*, but his name occurs in the magazine in 1901 and in the index for the first half of 1906 he appears as 'the late', which fits in with his death on January 30 that year.

The growth in the number of architectural books in the late 1890s and early 1900s, as well as Hudson's desire to enter that field, meant that it was necessary to find writers who would or could be specialists; and here he was singularly fortunate that H. Avray Tipping was prepared to take on houses as well as gardens.

H. Avray Tipping appears as such a formal, as well as important, figure in the history of *Country Life* that it is hard to imagine him playing the part of a pig in a village play and writing the piece himself. But the earliest printed work of his that I have found in the British Library is *A Hibernian Hyperbole entitled Three Ps or The Pig, the Paddy and the Patriot MP*, an elaborate title for a seventeen-page entertainment that he wrote and A.S. Pratt composed as the third part of an evening for the Primrose League in the Public Hall at Westerham on January 18, 1888.

Perhaps it should not have seemed so surprising, because at Oxford in the mid 1870s he had been a prominent member of OUDS, and Lady Congreve, a life-long friend of his, wrote a short Personal Recollection of him in which she said: 'He was very fond of getting up plays for village charities.' *The Hyperbole* was about Home Rule, and that fits too, because Lady Congreve remembered: 'A man who was a great friend of his when he was about thirty told me that he knew more about political economy than anyone in England and that it was a thousand pities he would not stand for Parliament. . . . He could be most amusing – how amusing it is difficult to put into words, because he made me laugh by his incisive

28. *Mathern Palace, Monmouthshire in 1910. Here Henry Avray Tipping laid out his first garden and also restored the house*

manner of speech and unusual way of expressing himself.'

Always a man of independent means, he began to garden seriously in the 1890s, and it was garden-making that led him into restoration and building, first at Mathern Palace (figs. 28, 117) in Monmouthshire and then nearby at Mounton (figs. 30, 141, 142, 143), where the urge to garden on a bigger scale led to a layout undertaken some ten years before beginning work on the new house; and then at High Glanau. Both houses were built with E.C. Francis, a local architect who had been a pupil of Dawber and an assistant of both Dawber and Blow. Almost inevitably his advice was sought by other people and occasionally he took on commissions; at Chequers, for instance, where he designed the architectural setting of the house in 1910-11; at Brinsop Court (figs. 139, 140), where he supervised the rescue of that house; and at Wyndcliffe Court, near Chepstow, where he designed a new garden for a new house in the 1920s.

However, he was not a man to choose a life of leisure, and for a number of years he worked on *The Dictionary of National Biography*. It was apparently through gardening that he came to know Hudson, and he appears first as the editor of *Country Life* books based on Charles Latham's photographs, *Gardens Old and New*, where he took over the second and third volumes, and then as editor of *In English Homes*. Throughout his life he continued to write almost as much about gardens as houses, although it is for his magisterial volumes on country houses that he is generally remembered, and it is probably significant that he did not become a Fellow of the Society of Antiquaries until 1909. As Christopher Hussey wrote after his death, 'If he had left behind him only the series of gardens that he made for himself between 1888 and

the present, excluding those he so much enjoyed laying out for friends,
he would have an honourable place amongst those who, during the past
half-century, have given English gardening the leading place it occupies
in the garden art of the Western world.'

His signed country house articles in the magazine start in 1907,
when he took over from C.J. Cornish, but that may well be misleading,
because there is a distinct interest in the work of Grinling Gibbons before
that as can be seen in the articles on Belton in 1903 and Petworth. I
suspect that is Tipping's, and the start of his book on Gibbons that
finally emerged in 1914.

Among the many frustrations caused by the vagueness of *Country Life's*
record-keeping is not knowing how or when Lawrence Weaver became
involved. His first signed articles on Lead Pipe Heads were published in
August and September, 1906, but it appears that a year earlier he wrote
about Earlshall in Fife (figs. 31, 88, 89, 90), the first restoration carried
out by Robert Lorimer and the key work in his Scottish practice.
Lorimer had known Gertrude Jekyll since she moved into Munstead

30. *The garden front of Mounton House, Monmouthshire in 1915. Tipping designed the house with the help of E.C. Francis*

Wood, if not earlier, and he also knew Lutyens, so it is possible that one or other of them could have talked about Weaver to Hudson. How the young Weaver came to write about Earlshall, however, is not recorded, and there is no clue as to whether it was Hudson's idea, Lorimer's or Weaver's, but it was to be the start of a varied and crucial contribution to *Country Life*.

Weaver began his training in an architect's office, but he did not complete it and he went to work for a firm which produced architectural leadwork. It was while working on their trade catalogue that he became interested in the history of leadwork and decided to write about it. In 1905 he flogged the subject quite hard, first in *The Architectural Review* and *The Burlington Magazine* and then in *Country Life*, finally producing his book on the subject in 1909. He joined the staff of *Country Life* as Architectural Editor in 1910.

He took charge of writing about new houses, particularly developing the series *The Lesser Country Houses of Today*. Presumably it was also under his influence that in 1909, 1910 and 1911 major articles were accorded to Home Place at Holt, by E.S. Prior; Standen, by

Philip Webb; Avon Tyrell, by W.R. Lethaby; Sandhouse at Witley in Surrey, by Reginald Blomfield; Nether Swell in Gloucestershire, by Guy Dawber; Ardenrun Place (figs. 32, 120, 121) in Surrey, by Ernest Newton; Crathorne in Yorkshire, by Ernest George; and Ardkinglas, Argyllshire by Lorimer.

There is little sense of *Country Life's* interest in new country house work (except for that of Lutyens, whom Hudson began to publicise in 1900) until Lawrence Weaver got going; and that is worth bearing in mind, given the picture painted by Roderick Gradidge in *Dream Houses* (1980). He regards the decade that saw the foundation of *Country Life* as a marvellously optimistic one when 'all the arts seemed to be moving to a minor Renaissance creating in the process a distinct English style' and one full of opportunity for younger architects in the field of houses in the country: 'Suddenly it seemed every one was building what they thought of as small houses, mostly in what is now called the stockbroker belt in Surrey, Sussex and Kent.'

In its first decade, however, *Country Life* played no part in making their work better known, and even Lutyens was receiving major commissions before *Country Life* published Crooksbury in 1900. Thus *Country Life's* broader influence on patronage was just starting to become established when the First World War broke out and destroyed the world from which those architects received big commissions.

The energy that Lawrence Weaver displayed in placing his leadwork articles is also apparent in the way he turned the material in his numerous *Country Life* articles on smaller houses (which were often published in the back of the paper and not bound into the volumes) into books. The first of these was *Small Country Houses of To-day*, published in 1910; the following year he produced *The House & Its Equipment*; and in 1912 he and Gertrude Jekyll produced *Gardens for Small Country Houses*. The authors had known each other since 1897, and the book appears to be a genuine joint production; and it is fascinating to see how they combined illustrations of historic examples and new work to create a total picture. In 1914 Lawrence Weaver produced another collection of *Small Country Houses*, which concentrated on *Their Repair and Enlargement. Forty Examples Chosen from Five Centuries*. He had been encouraged to write it by the particular interest shown in the seven chapters out of 48 in his *Small Country Houses of To-day* that dealt with repairs and enlarging. He pursued a careful line and, while he saw the year 1800 as the great divide, when 'the continuous development of tradition ceased, and building became the sport of eclectic fads in favour of one style or another,' he also wrote that he would 'protest as vigorously against the ill-treatment of a fine typical building by Pugin, Sir Charles Barry or Norman Shaw as against the loss of an eighteenth century house.'

If Weaver's main interest was in new buildings and craftsmanship he also occasionally wrote articles about historic houses, among those in 1912 being Moor Park, Hertfordshire, Claydon in Buckinghamshire, Wren House and Pallant House in Chichester and Castle Bromwich Hall in Warwickshire; but there is no apparent pattern in them.

Also he seems to have taken care of Scotland, producing a considerable

31. *Earlshall, Fife, in 1905. The first work of Robert Lorimer to be illustrated in* Country Life *and apparently the first article by Lawrence Weaver*

32. *Ardenrun Place, Surrey, by Ernest Newton. Built in 1906-09 it was illustrated in* Country Life *in 1911*

body of articles on historic houses, restoration and new work between 1912 and 1916. In 1912, for instance, he wrote about Falkland Palace, Balcaskie, Kinross, Winton, Fyvie and Midmar.

1913 saw the culmination of his early work in the special supplement in *Country Life* that he organised on Lorimer's work and the first edition of his book on *The Houses and Gardens of E.L. Lutyens*. In his preface to the latter he wrote: '. . . the debt which the twentieth century owes to the nineteenth and to such great architects as Norman Shaw, Eden Nesfield, George Devey and Philip Webb cannot be exaggerated. They relit the torch which is being carried on by a new generation of men, among whom Mr Lutyens fills a large place.' He also wrote: 'I may, perhaps, claim to have done something to enlarge public appreciation of the admirable houses, which are being built up and down the land, by illustrating and describing the work of nearly two hundred architects in the pages of *Country Life*.'

Weaver's influence was not just through his writing but through personal recommendation, as Clough Williams-Ellis explained in his short life of Weaver published in 1933: 'He was interested in all architects, but especially in younger ones showing the least animation, doing his utmost to get talent recognized whenever he found it, and giving criticism and advice in the most friendly and helpful fashion. . . . If by a little log-rolling or innocent wangling he could put a job in the way of talent, why, nothing could please him better; indeed it is difficult to say which gave him the most satisfaction, discovering and rewarding merit, seeing a job well done by the right man, or the actual lobbying or log-rolling that preceded and produced results so satisfying and so creditable to all concerned.'

If *Country Life's* direct influence on patronage took time to develop, it obviously quite quickly began to influence appreciation and taste through illustrating a wide range of historic examples, not only in general views but in superb detail, particularly of carving and plasterwork in houses like Belton (fig. 75), Coleshill (fig. 159), and Petworth.

Tipping understood that very clearly as he explained in an article he wrote in 1916 to mark the first thousand issues of *Country Life*: 'When *Country Life* first appeared the subject [of houses] was already attracting attention, there was a latent demand for correct and intelligent information.' It was a case of 'good seed falling on fertile soil. At first the pictures were delightful and the letterpress pleasant, but the educative influence was kept in reserve because it was necessary to begin homeopathically and only increase the dose as the tonic gave strength to the reader's system. . . . Each [house] has been so treated as to show some merit, teach some lesson, and exercise some influence on the taste of to-day.' That view contrasts with what Christopher Hussey wrote on *Country Life's* seventieth birthday in 1967. He saw the early years as tentative and experimental.

While Tipping and Weaver wrote the bulk of the articles, they had some assistance, as Tipping explained to Christopher Hussey in 1920. He mentioned Philip Mainwaring Johnstone, Herbert Kitchin and J.A. Gotch. All three were architects. Mainwaring Johnston, who was born in 1865, had been a pupil of Belcher and, as well as building houses, he restored both houses and churches and was interested in the preservation of wallpainting. He was also architect to Chichester Cathedral. *Who was Who* gives his recreations as 'antiquarian pursuits, photography, and gardening,' but made no mention of contributions to *Country Life*, most of which were on places in Sussex or Kent, among them a series on Arundel in and the article on Wardes in 1919.

George Herbert Kitchin (c.1870-1951), judging by his sketch books in the RIBA Drawings Collection, seems to have been a friend of Tipping and Gertrude Jekyll. The son of the Dean of Winchester, he practised as an architect in Winchester from 1903, working in an Arts and Crafts style. He also restored old buildings and seems to have laid out gardens, one of his principal commissions being at Lyegrove in Gloucestershire (*Country Life* December 14, 1929). Compton End, his cottage at Compton near Winchester, he described in *Country Life* on August 23, 1919.

The taste of *Country Life* in its first decade is apparent in the selection of houses in the three volumes of *In English Homes*. It was heavily slanted in favour of early houses, antiquity and great houses of noble families, but the treatment of houses dating from after 1740 was very uncertain, and

33. *The Romantic approach. A garden stairway at Hutton-in-the Forest, Cumberland, in 1907*

there was little real enthusiasm for houses like Nostell (fig. 99) or Newby. Nor was there much for recent houses, either, although The Deanery Garden (figs. 14, 17, 72, 73) appeared in Volume I and Clouds (figs. 83, 84, 85) and Marsh Court in Volume II. There were none in Volume III. That is itself interesting, because it underlines the need for Lawrence Weaver to write about them and give the magazine a better balance.

That *Country Life* was aware of that need is apparent from a remark in the Introduction to Volume II: 'We still flounder amid ill adapted copyings and misunderstood restorations; still lack the vigorous determination to give an honest and a living architectural setting to our moden mode of life, our modern domestic habits, customs and requirements.'

By 1911 it had become clear that the architectural articles of *Country Life* had developed a special importance, not least because they dealt with both the past and the present – the continuity of the British tradition, not just as a matter of academic interest but in relation to the formulation of a style suitable for that time. Moreover it was coming to be seen that what was topical was blending with a special form of recording. That it developed the second direction was due to the high standard of photography and the quality of Tipping's texts.

In 1912 Tipping added a fourth volume to Latham's *In English Homes* called *English Homes of the Early Renaissance*, on Elizabethan and Jacobean houses and gardens, which cost two guineas. It may have been the start of a new project, because the Country Notes page for January 7, 1922, said: 'But for some time before the war a far more formidable undertaking had been under consideration, namely to publish a series of volumes that would illustrate and be a repository of all that was important in English Domestic Architecture,' which could be seen sitting alongside Murray's *Dictionary of the English Language* and the *Dictionary of National Biography*. That would make sense, because from advertisements for current and forthcoming *Country Life* books at the back of Lawrence Weaver's *Small Country Houses of To-day* (1914) it is apparent that there was an ambitious programme in hand with his Lutyens and Tipping's Grinling Gibbons to be followed by *The Work of The Brothers Adam* by Arthur T. Bolton and *Decorative Plasterwork* by Laurence Turner, both of which are described as being in the press. The reference to the Adam book is particularly interesting because it ties up with his acknowledgements in Volume I of his *The Architecture of Robert and James Adam*, which finally came out in 1922: 'The first idea of the book was a simple one, a series of articles on the Brothers Adam to form a work uniform with the Architect's Library, which Sir Lawrence Weaver KBE had initiated.' The first article, Shardeloes, appeared in *Country Life* on July 5, 1913, and the last in 1921.

In 1916 *Country Life* reached its thousandth number and Tipping wrote a celebratory article, which suggested a much more conscious approach from the beginning that the magazine reveals or than Hussey recalled in 1970. As well as the remarks quoted on page 56 Tipping wrote: [by 1916] 'about 700 country houses of all styles and every size have been passed in review. But each one has been so treated as to show some merit, teach some lesson, and exercise some influence on the taste of today.' This

LANDSCAPES OF HELL
By Lieutenant Paul Nash.

DUNBARTON LAKES.

"One of the most dread places on the Western Front ; men never linger here. I have heard of some caught in a barrage amid this hollow unable to move back or forward for five hours. At night the mules use this "duck-board" track up to the line."

34. Landscapes of Hell. *An article published on January 19, 1918*

emphasis on the improvement of taste through historical example shows how closely the magazine was concerned with current architecture and how different was the world that it served from the situation after 1940 when the domestic movement of the previous fifty years came to an end. 'No wonder, then, that *Country Life* has become a document of great architectural importance . . . It is absolutely illuminating to the amateur, and gives hint and guidance to the many who propose to build or enlarge or alter or re-do their habitations and their gardens.'

If one looks through the issues of *Country Life* for 1914, the outbreak of war still makes a tremendous impression. Suddenly the magazine moved into a different gear. The aim was to keep up morale by combining as much as possible of the pre-war editorial content with many articles dealing with different aspects of the war effort, so that readers at home would never forget and those fighting would not feel forgotten. Moreover there were numerous articles on places abroad that were or might be threatened by the war, as well as others intended to emphasise links with allies. Thus the magazine appears both more practical and more outward looking.

Clearly great effort was put into maintaining the steady flow and the standard of the Country Home articles, which are the main concern here, but it is only right to suggest, albeit briefly, how the whole editorial effort was directed towards winning the war. Even the frontispiece was influenced by it: on August 15, 1914, for instance, the caption to the photograph of Lady Beatty mentioned her placing her yacht at the disposal of the Government for hospital purposes. Most of the leaders were inspired by it, and there were many articles on such subjects as 'Collecting Horses for the Army in a Hunting County' (August 15, 1914), 'A Day with Recruits in Belton Camp' (September 26, 1914), 'Public School and University Corps' (March 13, 1915). (Indeed the interest in OTCs led to the establishment of the *Country Life* Rifle Shooting Competition as early as 1912). There were series on 'What the Country Gentleman Has Done for the War' and 'Sportsmen and the War', taken county by county and illustrated with photographs of serving officers. Articles were sent in on 'Birds and Beasts at the Fighting Front' (January 29, 1915) and 'Birds Nesting at the Front' (May 6, 1916), and alongside them were 'Field Ambulance Work in Gallipoli' (January 15, 1915) and 'Landscapes of Hell by Lieutenant Paul Nash' on January 18, 1918. Even now the mixture is deeply moving.

Most of the architectural writing had to be done by Tipping, who obviously had increasing difficulty in organising geographical variety as the war went on year after year. In 1917, for instance, there was a heavy concentration of places in Shropshire, perhaps because he was able to arrange them from his home in Monmouthshire.

He was able to call on help from Arthur Bolton, who had begun work on his Adam book just before the War and continued to contribute articles, among them West Wycombe and Hatchlands in 1916. Presumably his architectural practice had gone to nothing, and the *Country Life* connection was useful until he took over Sir John Soane's Museum in 1917. Martin Conway, who was already a friend of Hudson and Tipping, also lent a hand. He was a neighbour of Hudson in Queen Anne's Gate and in his memoirs, *Episodes in a Varied Life*, published by *Country Life* in 1932, he refers to him as 'my excellent friend'. Some of his contributions were straight Country Home articles, as on Knowlton Court, Kent, in 1916, and Wollaton Hall, Nottingham, in 1917, and on his own work at Allington Castle in Kent in 1918.

His field, however, was broader than that, because he was deeply concerned about the possible destruction of places and art treasures abroad, among them Torcello in 1916. There were also some odd articles that are a reminder of what a different world it was: on April 24th, 1915 he published one called 'The Palaces of the Warring Rulers' with illustrations of the Royal Palace in Brussels, the Elysée, Peterhof, Windsor, the Kaiser's Palace in Potsdam, the Hofburg and the Sultan's Palace at Constantinople.

Lawrence Weaver appears less frequently than might be expected, and it is conceivable that he began his war work well before 1916, when, after a period cleaning latrines at the White City and working as a clerk, he was introduced by Lord Riddell to Sir Arthur Lee and entered the Ministry of Food. However, he continued to write occasional signed articles on country houses. On June 6, 1917 he wrote 'What Architects Have Done in the War' and that may have prompted a tribute to Alwyn Ball, who was killed in 1916, in the form of an article on Houndstall House (now Houndsell Place), Sussex, by his former employers A.D. Smith and Cecil Brewer (February 2, 1918). Weaver may well have written a number of the leaders in *Country Life*, but, alas, there is no record of who did what.

One of the surprises is to find so many articles on French chateaux: presumably they had been photographed by Frederick H. Evans long before, in preparation for Theodore Andrea Cook's book *Twenty Five Great Houses of France*, which bears no publication date but was reviewed in *Country Life* on January 20, 1917.

Another surprise is the first sign of interest in American architecture, in particular in the houses of Charles Platt, about which Samuel Howe wrote on May 6, 1916, January 13, 1917 and May 18, 1918. Much of the issue of June 23, 1917, was devoted to 'An Appreciation of America', a follow-up of an earlier issue on Italy that was clearly prompted by the war effort.

With the end of the War *Country Life* speedily changed gear again, as can be seen from the contents of December 7, 1918. Starting with a leader on 'Our Housing Policy', surely prompted or written by Lawrence Weaver, it went on to 'The Recreation of Gardens' by Gertrude Jekyll, 'The Future of Fox Hunting', 'Shooting after the War', 'The Re-Birth of Racing', 'The Revival of Cricket' and 'The Future of Gun Dogs', a trug of *Country Life* chestnuts.

Country Life came through the First World War remarkably unchanged as far as its aims and balance was concerned, but, as it approached its twenty-fifth year, it was natural that Edward Hudson should start looking for a younger generation to carry on the magazine; and again it shows his gifts as a patron that, with Tipping's aid, he found people who were to serve *Country Life* for such a long time. First came A.E. Henson (figs. 37, 38), the principal photographer from 1917 to 1957; Christopher Hussey, who became a member of the editorial staff in 1921 and was to be the main driving force on the architectural side for over thirty years and continued to write regularly until his death in 1970; C.H. Reilly, the Professor of Civic Design at Liverpool University, who had a formal arrangement with the magazine in the early 1920s; Ralph Edwards, who concentrated on the history of English furniture from 1921 to 1926 before he went to the Victoria and Albert Museum. Then, in 1928, came Arthur Oswald, who remained a member of the staff, except during the war when he served in the Navy, until he retired in 1969. They all contributed greatly to the character and development of the magazine.

In the early 1920s Hudson and Tipping were, of course, still the main figures, and they remained so until the early 1930s, when Tipping died and Hudson was forced to become less active through ill health. Of their relationship at that time a glimpse has been left by Ralph Edwards, who wrote: 'On Tipping's visits to the office he would burst into the board room like a tornado, and Hudson would be instantly transformed from a dictator into an obedient slave.' He was a 'veritable oracle in the eyes of Edward Hudson.' Of Tipping himself Edwards wrote: 'Blind in one eye, if anything put him out, he could, with the other, look very ferocious. He was of powerful physique and active mind, genial (until crossed), supremely self-confident and resolutely determined to get his own way.'

Tipping continued to develop his historical interests, as can be seen particularly clearly in the series of English Homes published by *Country Life*

35. *Plumpton Place, Sussex. The inner front of the cottages at the entrance designed by Lutyens for Edward Hudson in 1928*

36. *The Mill House at Plumpton at the end of the lower lake. Edward Hudson lived here while planning to restore the manor house*

after the war, but he was no longer young in 1918 and not surprisingly he showed little or no interest in new developments in architecture.

In a book of this kind, when the illustrations are the real point, it is a happy coincidence that it is possible to start on the second generation with its principal photographer, who continued to be so until he retired in 1957. A.E. Henson's contribution is the unsung one, because, unlike Charles Latham, he did not produce books, or have books produced in

his name, and his name was never acknowledged in the magazine.

He was a perfectionist, who worked slowly, as can be seen from the photograph showing him making elaborate but not untypical preparations to take the Great Hall at Rufford Old Hall (fig. 38) in 1929; and in later life he was quite a crusty and difficult character. He did not drive a car and was a scourge of house-keepers and butlers, who were still in plentiful supply during most of his working life. Elaborate progresses had to be arranged for him every year whereby he concentrated on one or two areas. The electric current had to be checked in advance because it was so varied, if not non-existent; the household had to be on hand to pull blinds as required and move quantities of furniture; lawns had to be removed if the lines ran the wrong way, and branches – and even, once, a tree – had

38. *A.E. Henson preparing to photograph the great hall at Rufford Old Hall, Lancashire, in 1929*

to be felled when they were in the way of his compositions. After 1939, when there were fewer or no servants, owners were made to co-operate, as can be gathered from Lady Meade-Fetherstonhaugh's account of his visit to Uppark in 1941: ' . . . complete with bowler hat on a lovely summer morning he stood in the Park waving a handkerchief – a signal that Lady Wolverton was to pull up the window blinds, which she was loath to do . . . and by his quiet kind insistence he had me & the butler & the Chauffeur & my maid completely victimized, & he had a Dark Room rigged in "Mr Weaver's closet" . . . and rigged so completely and in so short a time . . .' He, like Alex Starkey, was very particular that a house should not look dead or blind when he photographed its exterior.

One owner came home to find all the glasses in the house laid out on

39. *The result of the preparations. The interior of the great hall at Rufford*

the grass: it was a dull day, and Henson wanted to increase the amount of light reflected back into the rooms he was photographing. Others, I believe, found the windows blacked out with Buckingham Palace writing paper given to him by Queen Mary. The Queen had a great respect for him, and immediately after the death of King George V she asked whether he could be spared to record the private rooms at Buckingham Palace before they were disturbed. When he went to photograph Scotney Castle for Christopher Hussey soon after he inherited in 1952, Henson shook his head: now Mr Hussey wanted all the furniture included that for years he had been asked to remove from sight.

His method of work has been described by Fred Harden, who started work at *Country Life* in 1921 at the age of seventeen-and-a-half and retired in 1968. Apparently he always demanded a room in a house, because 'if a photograph did not come too well, he could take another right away. One of the photographers once said: 'He doesn't use an exposure meter, he uses a bottle of developer.' Thus when he returned to his house at Wootton Wawen, Birmingham, he had all his negatives ready for printing. 'All his early prints were in sepia because they were printed in daylight; the negatives were put in a frame with paper (I think it was called Seltona) and exposed to sunlight/daylight. This took longer than B and W printing but he had plenty of time as all his developing had been done at the Country Houses.'

Of the other photographers who contributed to the Country Homes series unfortunately nothing much appears to be known except their names, which survive through appearing on the backs of prints or on batches of negatives. I have found Ward on the back of an interior of 15 Queen Anne's Gate; Arthur Tedman took the post-fire photographs of Sledmere; F.W. Westley took the series of photographs at Marchmont; while Frank Sleigh was on the staff from 1922 to 1925. Arthur Gill, who was brought from Hudson and Kearns to help on the *Dictionary of Furniture* and later did the great series of Delhi, photographed the Long Gallery at Penheale. Sometimes Henson and one of the other photographers divided the work on a large house or a complicated job, Westley and Gill being particularly good at furniture; but it is a comment on Hudson's eye and control that there is so little variation in quality visible to a layman.

Turning to writers, C.H. Reilly was already a well established figure in the world of architecture when he began to contribute to *Country Life* in 1921. Born in 1874 and trained in the office of John Belcher, he became Professor of Architecture at Liverpool University so was more important as a teacher than a practitioner. From 1904 he was involved with journalism, which, as he explained in *Scaffolding in the Sky*, he saw as a proper extension of teaching. He also described how in 1922 he was putting in a day a week at *Country Life* at Lord Riddell's suggestion: 'He fancied I could provide that paper with ideas and I was appointed nominally Architectural Editor. I did provide ideas, or thought I did, in large numbers but it was not till I left the paper that I began to see some of them, like an interest in modern design and in what the theatre was doing, creeping in.'

He had a special interest in American architecture, particularly Beaux Arts classicism, and his first article in *Country Life* was a review of the Modern American Architecture exhibition at the RIBA on November 26, 1921; and on February 18, 1922 he wrote about 'The City of Washington and American Architecture'. However most of his articles were about public architecture and public buildings in Britain, starting with a series on 'London Streets and Their Recent Buildings', which began on May 22, 1922. The idea for them grew out of earlier series that he had written on Liverpool and Manchester for the *Liverpool Daily Post* and the *Guardian*; but as he wrote, 'The *Country Life* series, after nine had appeared, came to a sudden stop. The Editor did not like my remarks about the building of one of his chief advertisers. After all, editors are human except those of the *Manchester Guardian*.'

Reilly's connection with *Country Life* raises again another aspect of the paper and those involved with it, its role in connection with patronage. It is impossible to know how many architects received commissions directly or indirectly through the magazine, because so few are documented. It is known that Lutyens got several jobs either through the magazine or as a result of Hudson's recommendation, and, as Gavin Stamp pointed out in 'The Rise and Fall and Rise of Edwin Lutyens' in *The Architectural Review* in 1981, 'It did not matter that the architectural journals at first gave him less coverage, for *Country Life* introduced him to potential clients rather than architects.'

In his autobiography Reilly explained how one major commission came his way: 'I had written a picturesque article for *Country Life* suggesting that the new buildings for London University should be on the river, like so many of London's finest monuments, and I had suggested for them the land between the House of Lords and the Tate Gallery. King's College also wanted a new site and Doulton's works on the south bank was said to be in the market. I suggested King's College should move there and Lambeth Bridge, about to be rebuilt by Sir Reginald Blomfield, should be called University Bridge as it should connect the two groups of university buildings. I saw processions of graduates in their gowns and brightly coloured hoods passing from one side to the other. Anyway, the idea made an amusing article I think. It was never published, but I was paid for it many times over. Edward Hudson, the Editor of *Country Life*, handed over the proof to his friend J.B. Stevenson, the managing director of the great firm of Messrs Holland and Hannen and Cubitts, who, it appeared, owned the land on which I proposed to plant the University. He was very struck with my idea and I was asked to a luncheon by Hudson to meet him.' That led to Stevenson asking him to do Devonshire House, of which he owned the site: 'We think the right thing to do,' he said, 'is to build an American apartment house upon it, costing about two millions. It is very important we should get the right American architect for the job. You, I believe, know them all. Will you give me the names of six of their leading men and their qualifications.'

Reilly recommended Thomas Hastings, and Stevenson offered the commission to Hastings as a joint one with Reilly.

Another good illustration of about the same date was provided by the late Paul Paget, who opened his office with his partner, John Seely, in 1926. John Seely's father had inherited Mottistone Manor (fig. 40) in the Isle of Wight and had asked the two young men to restore it, but before they started work, he sought the advice of Lutyens, who was a close friend. Lutyens not only approved their sketch plans but 'alerted his "Fidus Achetus" [sic] Edward Hudson to see whether the result was any good.' And so Hudson came to Mottistone with Christopher Hussey; 'and on March 16, 1929, Christopher Hussey wrote about the house in *Country Life*.'

40. *Mottistone Manor, Isle of Wight, as restored by John Seely and Paul Paget. It was illustrated in 1929*

As a result of reading that article Sir Neville Pearson, who was a director of *Country Life* and was then married to Gladys Cooper, the actress, asked them to overhaul and replan 1 and 2 The Grove, Highgate Village. Publication of that work led to yet more commissions including a steady flow in Highgate that lasted until Paul Paget's retirement in 1969.

While C.H. Reilly was recruited to write about new buildings, Ralph Edwards, who was a generation younger, was brought on to the staff in 1921 to write about furniture. He was recruited by Tipping, 'having come into contact with him through writing a laudatory review of the first volume of *English Homes*. He was extremely susceptible to judicious flattery.' As Ralph Edwards explained, 'I was looking around for some congenial, and by the standards then obtaining sufficiently remunerative job' and Hudson took him 'on the understanding that I should contribute articles, subsequently to form part of the raw material for Percy's [Macquoid] darling and long-cherished project for a *Dictionary*.' Macquoid for his part agreed that the writing should be done by Ralph Edwards. Hudson was determined that the project should not be blocked by the costs involved, and eventually *The Dictionary of English Furniture* appeared in three volumes between 1924 and 1927 as a joint work of Macquoid and Edwards. Percy Macquoid died soon after the first volume was finished, leaving only fragmentary material, but Hudson wanted the rest of the *Dictionary* to appear under his name. Much of Macquoid's research had been done by his wife Theresa, so Ralph Edwards completed the two succeeding volumes in collaboration with her.

The business of producing the *Dictionary* was an enormous task and from the beginning a number of contributors were called on to write particular entries. In Volume I Tipping wrote the general introduction and Ingleson Goodison, John C. Rogers, Margaret Jourdain and W.G. Thomson were also involved. In Volume II they were joined by Oliver Brackett, John Seymour Lindsay, and H. Clifford Smith. In Volume III the new names were those of Canon Francis W. Galpin and W.A. Propart.

Although the *Dictionary* surveyed the subject from mediaeval times down to the late Georgian period, it concentrated on the years from about 1690 to 1810, so forming part of the resurrection of the eighteenth century in which *Country Life* played such an active role in the 1920s and 1930s.

Altogether Ralph Edwards spent five years at *Country Life*, and he continued to write articles for many years after that. Also he published several other books with *Country Life*.

It took a little time after the end of the war for *Country Life* to revive its pre-war plans for book publication, but, as well as the *Dictionary* project, it pressed on with the revival of Tipping's idea of a monumental successor to Latham's *In English Homes*. Between 1920 and 1937 it managed to bring out nine folio volumes, of which the two on the eighteenth century appear today to be the most original. Because the numbering is confusing all the titles are given here.

Period I Volume I Norman and Plantaganet (1921); Period II Volume I Early Tudor (1929); Period I and I Volume II Mediaeval and Early Tudor (1936); Period III Volume I Late Tudor and Early Stuart (1922); Period III Volume II Late Tudor and Early Stuart (1927); Period IV Volume I Late Stuart (1920); Period IV Volume II The Work of Sir John Vanbrugh and his School (1928); Period V Volume I Early Georgian (1921); Period VI Volume I Late Georgian (1926).

Among other important books were Bolton's long promised study of Robert and James Adam, which finally appeared in two volumes in 1922, and *Buckingham Palace* (1931) by H. Clifford Smith, with a historical introduction and architectural description by Christopher Hussey, an early appreciation of Nash and one of the first books attempting to deal in detail with architecture and contents.

The crucial appointment of those years was that of Christopher Hussey in 1921. Not only did he make the most remarkable contribution to *Country Life* over a period of fifty years, but he is a very interesting figure because of the way his thinking developed in so many interlocking directions. However in order to appreciate his contribution it is necessary to understand his background. Indeed it is a story that explains a great deal about *Country Life*, its stability and success over the past seventy years and the values that it continues to stand for. So it also throws light on certain aspects of English life and thought. Christopher Hussey was that rare figure, a practical philosopher, an intellectual Whig, and he could draw strength from his background to work with great industry on a front much broader than appears from a cursory examination of his articles.

Meeting Christopher Hussey for the first time in the old *Country Life* office in Tavistock Street could be a rather intimidating experience, especially on Fridays when he wanted to get his leader completed. If, however, one saw him at home in later years at Scotney Castle, on the border of Kent and Sussex, he appeared in a very different light: a decidedly cheerful-looking man who seemed to enjoy everything he did, whether it was retiring to his study to get on with whatever he was writing (he had impressive powers of concentration and production), or considering improvements to the garden, or replanting in the park, or making plans for modernising cottages, or choosing a bull for his herd of Sussex cattle, or singing lustily in church, or driving with rather too much brio to see some neighbouring garden, or giving sound opinions on the Historic Buildings Council, or seeing friends at the Garrick Club.

It was at Scotney, which he inherited at the age of fifty-three, that he combined his intellectual life with that of being a country squire, and what was so fascinating was to see how his whole approach grew out of the place and the ideas that influenced his grandfather as a young man in the 1830s. His grandfather, Edward Hussey , who was born in 1807, had been brought up on, or discovered for himself, late eighteenth-century theories of landscape, gardening and architecture. These found expression in his creation, in the mid 1830s, of the landscape round the ruins of the old castle at Scotney (fig. 42), and the building of the new house by Salvin which looked down to the ruins.

Christopher Hussey, being the son of a younger son, albeit the likely heir from an early age, was not brought up at Scotney; but from the age of twelve he generally went to stay with his uncle and aunt every Easter. His visits were neither frequent, nor, it seems, particularly enjoyable, but the place came to mean a great deal to him, even if he did not fully understand the theories that influenced his grandfather until he was in his early twenties. As he wrote to his future wife after he had taken her there for the first time at the end of 1935: 'It was such an adventure – taking you to Scotney. And a wholly successful one. That scene, you know, means a lot to me – background, retreat, never-never land; and I am shy of showing it to people in case they hurt me by reacting wrongly.'

Both his parents painted competently, as had his grandparents and his parental great grandmother, and it was they who opened his eyes. Frequently they stayed at Stoke Edith, a house for which he developed a particularly deep feeling, and most summers they took a house in the country for a few weeks, when there were opportunities to visit houses and churches. He was to dedicate *The Picturesque* 'To my Father and Mother who early instructed me in the principles of the Picturesque'.

He inherited their pleasure in painting, his work forming an almost complete chronicle of his life from 1909, when he was at his private school at Broadstairs, through his years at Eton, where he won the drawing prize in 1917, to be most fully expressed in the long series of watercolours of houses that he and his wife stayed in after their marriage.

His main spare-time activities, however, to begin with, were the theatre and journalism. He put on his first play in his parents' house just before Christmas, 1912, and as soon as he got to Eton he became involved in acting, stage managing, writing and producing, developing in the process

CRUSE

EFFECT

The charming Mr Tipping
Had The strange habit of slipping
Into any old house, so to speak, unawares
And Then tearing up stairs.

When expelled from The residence
major Hussey offered evidence
(in The shape of a coin which I think was
refused)
and at The same Time was severely
abused.

41. *H. Avray Tipping as seen by Christopher Hussey about 1915*

a life-long delight in Gilbert and Sullivan. His extraordinary facility was often demonstrated when he wrote office pantomimes for *Country Life* in the 1930s. That writing always came easily to him is apparent from a letter to Ralph Dutton written shortly after he joined up in 1919: 'You have probably discovered before now I am actuated to write letters by the same passion that makes people enjoy hearing their own voice.' In fact writing came more easily than talking, because he had an impediment in his speech that troubled him, particularly at school, where he often found it difficult to give his name; and which made his pleasure in performing all the more remarkable.

Of his early journalistic enterprises at Eton, and then at Oxford, there is plenty of evidence, starting with the third number of a magazine called *The Lucky Sixpence*, dated July 15, 1915. Then in 1917 he started a paper called *The Red Cross*, which indirectly led to his first contribution to *Country Life*, published on November 10, 1917; an article called 'The Public School on the Land'. That came about because P. Anderson Graham, the Editor, wrote to the Headmaster asking for an article on work done at harvest and other camps by public schools, to be written by a member of staff or a boy.

However, the *Country Life* connection came about not through that article but through H. Avray Tipping's being a friend of his parents and a frequent visitor to their house in Hereford Gardens, Park Lane. As can be seen from a caricature done by Christopher Hussey in about 1915 (fig. 41), he was a familiar figure. As soon as Christopher Hussey left school in the spring of 1918 he joined up. He was due to go to France on September 18, but at the last moment that was cancelled, and then in November came the Armistice. Then, as his sister Barbara Birley remembered, one evening when she was standing in the drawing room at Hereford Gardens, 'Tipping suddenly swept up the stairs and into the room. "Mary," he said, "I want that boy for *Country Life*. He must go at once to Oxford, try for a first and then he will come straight into *Country Life* – while he is there he can try his hand at articles during the vacation."'

At Oxford Christopher Hussey devoted a good deal of time to the theatre, writing and producing, and to journalism, starting a paper called *The Cardinal's Hat* with Noel Carrington as well as refloating various societies that had been dormant during the War. Even so his tutors thought that he ought to get a first, and they, at least, were disappointed that he just missed one, writing to say that the examiners were divided and that anyway he should try for All Souls that autumn. Tipping had been as good as his word and organised his first articles while he was at Oxford. In April, 1920, he stayed at Scotney for ten days, his first long visit there, and it was there that he must have worked out his first three articles on Scotney, Finchcocks and Old Wilsey at Cranbrook.

The only surviving letter to him from Tipping, which starts 'My dear Christopher', is dated June 6, 1920, and sets out the terms of working for *Country Life*. '*Country Life* pays from 2 to 5 guineas per 1000 words and it would seem not out of the way for you just at first to begin at the bottom, but I have arranged that you shall be on the 3 guinea scale. As a matter of fact I am on that, but then the payment to me for contributions is really subsidiary to my editorial fee, and it is only because of the latter that I have never asked to be put down on the 5 guinea scale, which is an innovation due to present prices. Please note however that payment is inclusive and the contributors do not charge travelling expenses for visiting the places. That is why they are best arranged somewhat in districts or in the regions where the contributor lives or largely works, hence Mainwaring Johnston generally does Sussex, Herbert Kitchin Hampshire, Gotch Northamptonshire, only of late times they have all been lazy and I have had to do nearly the whole thing.'

Christopher Hussey joined the editorial staff in 1921 and that year his contributions include Finchcocks, a group of five articles on Eton, four on York and on the Abbey House at Barrow in Furness. The York articles can be traced back to a visit in 1919 of which there are records in his sketch books. The article on Abbey House was his first one on a Lutyens building: that was done because he had wanted to have a trip to the North the previous year and Avray Tipping had suggested doing a group of places. As far as Hudson was concerned that was another Lutyens building in the bag, but for Christopher Hussey it was the first in what became a favourite theme that was to continue for the rest of his life, his last articles in 1970 including two on the Master.

The article is also interesting because it shows how he had picked up an essential thread in Tipping's and Weaver's work before the War – the search for a style for today. At the end he wrote, 'the brilliance of the design lies in the fact that the house satisfies both schools of thought in that it is essentially Jacobean and undeniably Lutyens. And in this elasticity of style lies, I think, the great hope of modern architecture.'

One puzzling question is when Christopher Hussey actually discovered the Picturesque as an aesthetic theory. In his book he writes vividly of his discovery in the library at Scotney. 'The picturesque was the artistic tradition in which I was brought up, and I remember clearly the shock with which I suddenly became conscious that it was only one of the many aspects of reality. On this particular evening I was pondering on the happy chance, as it appeared to me, of my grandfather's desertion of the old castle, his building of the new house on this particular spot, and his digging of the stone for building it between the two - in the quarry that makes such a fine foreground to the prospect. It did not occur to me that he was guided by anything more than chance and natural good taste. At that point, however, my eye, ranging the mellow shelves beside me, fell on the book that Henry Tilney had been reading at Bath, *Sir Uvedale Price on the Picturesque*. What was "the Picturesque"? And what could be found to say on it filling so fat a volume? It was humiliating, at the time, to find my aesthetic impulses no more than the product of heredity and environment.'

Everything is there but the date. His first article on Scotney is purely about the old castle and does not touch on its Picturesque significance, which it surely would have done if he had been aware of the literary background to what his grandfather had done. So I think that his discovery must have taken place a little later, about 1924. The first full exposition of the Picturesque in his writings is in his article on Dunglass (fig. 43), near Haddington, which he published on September 12, 1925. His opening paragraph suggests a fresh excitement at his discovery of Uvedale Price, as if he had recently read him. Clearly the setting of Dunglass made a great impression on him, and that explains a photograph of it in *The Picturesque*.

Unfortunately Christopher Hussey did not keep a diary, although his engagement books exist, and he never wrote any memoirs, although he was considering the possibility at the time of his death. However, from his engagements and the visiting albums it is possible to see how his friendships and his regular writing for *Country Life* interlocked. Among his friends who were significant in that respect were Colonel Cooper, who had a passion for restoring old houses and lived in four, three of which Christopher Hussey wrote about in *Country Life*, Cold Ashton (figs. 189-191) in Gloucestershire, Cothay in Somerset, Julians in Hertfordshire (which he left before there was time to get it photographed) and Knightstone. Reggie Cooper was a friend of people such as Lord Gerald Wellesley, Lawrence Johnston, Norah Lindsay and Sybil Colefax.

A number of his articles came about through friendships and family connections, but a little more needs to be said about how the general programme of articles was put together and how and why his writing

42. *Scotney Castle Kent. The view from the house over the quarry to the old castle in 1956*

took the form it did. There has always had to be variety in the houses described, with geographical spread and differences of character, period and scale all taken into account, and small houses described in a single article mixed with those requiring two or three. At the same time the office's refusal to pay writers' travelling expenses had to be taken into account, as had writers' plans for books. Thus what might appear a comparatively straightforward operation has always been a kind of juggling, and I am sure that over the years it has frequently looked as if all the balls would fall at the same moment, leaving no article to put in.

This helps to explain why the number of threads that Christopher Hussey was pursuing in any five-year period seems baffling to some one not involved. Once he had played himself in, in 1920 and 1921, various groups of articles can be identified. In 1922 the photographer was sent to do a round of houses in Rutland, Nottinghamshire, Derbyshire and

43. *A picturesque composition. Dunglass, Haddington. An illustration from an article by Christopher Hussey in 1935 that suggests his recent discovery of the Picturesque*

possibly Cheshire too; and as a result in 1923 he wrote about Burley-on-the-Hill in Rutland, Clifton, Nuthall Temple, Thrumpton and also Ednaston, a new Lutyens house, all in Nottinghamshire; Foremark, towards the Derbyshire-Leicestershire border; and Tabley and Winnington in Cheshire. Discussions must also have been going on with Tipping about the projected Vanbrugh volume of English Homes, so he wrote about Seaton Delaval in 1923, Grimsthorpe in 1924 and Eastbury and Kings Weston in 1927. At the same time there was a group of Lutyens buildings to be published: thus in addition to Ednaston, he wrote on Folly Farm, the Queen's Dolls' House (figs. 44, 181-186), the Midland Bank in Piccadilly and Government House, India. Most years he had one big project: in 1921/22 six articles on Eton, which were republished in book form, and eight on York and houses in the city; in 1923 five articles on Bramshill; in 1924/25 four on Kensington Palace; and in 1925 five

44. *The Queen's dolls house being packed up in Lutyens's house, 13 Mansfield Street*

on Petworth, which again were published in book form. The elaboration of architectural history and the growth of archival research since the Second War has made that kind of pace difficult to sustain, but even in those simpler days it was constantly amazing that Christopher Hussey got through so much while at the same time developing his thinking about broader themes.

Christopher Hussey's discovery of the Picturesque was of cardinal importance in the development of an intellectual approach that extended far beyond his interest in country houses to the history of landscape design, the role of architecture in landscape, and so to the problems of modern architecture, landscape design, planning and preservation. So it is surely remarkable that about the time he read Sir Uvedale Price on the Picturesque, he should have read the original French edition of Le

Corbusier's *Vers une architecture*. It is possible that he bought the latter as soon as it came out, and certainly the underlinings of his now very battered copy suggest a careful reading.

He already took a progressive view of architecture, as can be seen in his article on Abbey House at Barrow, and in 1922 he had been one of the founder members of the Architecture Club. In March, 1923, it held its first exhibition, largely through the support of *Country Life* and presumably the hard work of Christopher Hussey. He wrote about it on March 10 and 17; and in 1924 he reviewed its second exhibition and also the Architectural Room at the Royal Academy. He also gave a paper to the 63 Club in the session of 1924-25 on 'Mechanics or Architecture' that must have related to his reading of *Vers une architecture*.

It is not clear whether Christopher Hussey went to see the Paris exhibition in 1925, but it led him to join up with a group of contemporaries enthusiastic about modern design who planned to hold an exhibition in London. Among those involved were Chermayeff and Etchells, the translator of *Vers une architecture* in 1927. Nothing came of the project, but Christopher Hussey did not lose sight of it and eventually he brought it to fruition in 1933 in an exhibition of Industrial Art at Dorland Hall.

Country Life had published an article on the Unit concrete cottage at Braintree by W.F. Crittall and C.H.B. Quennell as early as November 8, 1919, conceivably as a result of prompting from Lawrence Weaver, who was still a director of the company. But Hudson would not have looked with favour on Christopher Hussey's interest in Le Corbusier or the new continental architecture. There are, however, a few signs in the magazine, among them an article on 'The Steel House' in January, 1925 and a leader on 'The Concrete House' three weeks later. Then in 1928 there started to be a trickle, with a perspective of Tait's new houses at Braintree and an article on Tait's houses at Silver End Village: the first Modern Movement houses in Britain to receive full coverage.

Clearly Christopher Hussey was aware of what was going on abroad, although he had little opportunity to travel except on his annual holiday. He went to look at new building in Cologne in 1928 on the way back from a tour of Bavaria with Roger and Peter Hesketh, and he went again to Germany in 1930 and 1931. In a letter to Billa Cresswell, now Lady Harrod, he wrote: 'Keep your eyes open for the modern German architecture. It is intensely interesting. We have nothing to compare with it here. Of course judged by classic or picturesque, or any other standards, it is "ugly". But so is everything else new. Often it is highly effective & sometimes thrillingly adventurous. The great thing is that it is *serviceable* and expresses the spirit of today. Whether it is architecture is another thing . . . ' The same year (1931) he wrote about High and Over (figs. 13, 222, 223, 224). Also John Summerson came to *Country Life* with the idea of editing a new magazine, but the idea came to nothing and after he had written a number of articles including a review of a Victorian exhibition, and on Vincent Harris's work in 1934, he left to edit *The Architect and Building News*.

1931 saw an upheaval in Christopher Hussey's domestic arrangements.

45. *Valewood, Sussex. Oliver Hill's weekend house that he shared with Christopher Hussey in the early 1930s*

He had continued to live during the week in his parents' house, by then in Cadogan Square, but for some years he had shared a small week-end house in Buckinghamshire with Lord Gerald Wellesley. Suddenly Lord Gerald decided to give it up, and it was then that Oliver Hill asked whether he would like to share Valewood (figs. 45, 268, 269, 270), near Dorking. It is hard to think of people more unalike than Lord Gerald and Oliver Hill, but Christopher Hussey was able to appreciate both, so the arrangement over Valewood lasted very happily until he married in 1936.

Oliver Hill was a great enthusiast and as a result of their complementary interests in modern architecture, together they resurrected Christopher Hussey's long-held desire to have an exhibition. There had been increasing disquiet about British standards of industrial design as well as the serious economic consequences that resulted, and both were brought home by the success of the Stockholm Exhibition of Modern Industrial and Decorative Art held in 1930. As a result of that an exhibition of Swedish Industrial Arts and Crafts was held at Dorland Hall in 1931 (which Christopher Hussey reviewed in *Country Life*), and that led to the establishment of a committee under Lord Gorell to consider the relations between art and industry and to advise the Board of Trade about exhibitions. Together they led to the idea of an exhibition of British industrial art (fig. 46) for which Christopher Hussey obtained *Country Life's* blessing and financial support in 1930. That forms the background to numerous articles: on the new BBC building, when Christopher Hussey illustrated the work of McGrath, Maufe, Chermayeff and Wells Coates; Oswald Milne's additions to Claridges; and Gayfere House, Westminster, which Oliver Hill had designed for Lord and Lady Mount Temple, all published in 1932.

All except Maufe were involved with the exhibition. Christopher Hussey was chairman and also a personal guarantor; Frank Pick was deputy chairman, and Noel Carrington and Paul Nash were among those on the committee. How significant an event the exhibition, which was held at Dorland Hall, Regent Street, from June 20 to July 12 proved to be must be for a historian of the 1930s to decide, but it did include

Chermayeff's week-end house and Wells Coates' Minimum Flat, a replica of one of the Isokan flats then rising in Lawn Road, Hampstead.

After it closed Wells Coates wrote to Christopher Hussey: 'I am sure that all of us who were in the "inner circle" of the organisation of the Exhibition of British Industrial Art appreciate the qualities of generalship which you displayed as Chairman. It has been a difficult year, and I am sure that the success of this first selective Exhibition in England will make it easier for those who know that the same ideals must be carried further, through every possible channel. For my part, I hope that the next Exhibition of this sort will be another stepping stone of sound contemporary British design.' In fact a second exhibition was held the following year, but Christopher Hussey was not involved: Oliver Hill was the moving spirit.

Naturally the 1933 exhibition was reviewed at length – by Arthur Oswald, whose heart was never in that kind of thing – but that article is part of a carefully orchestrated group.

In February Christopher Hussey wrote about High Cross Hill (fig. 48)

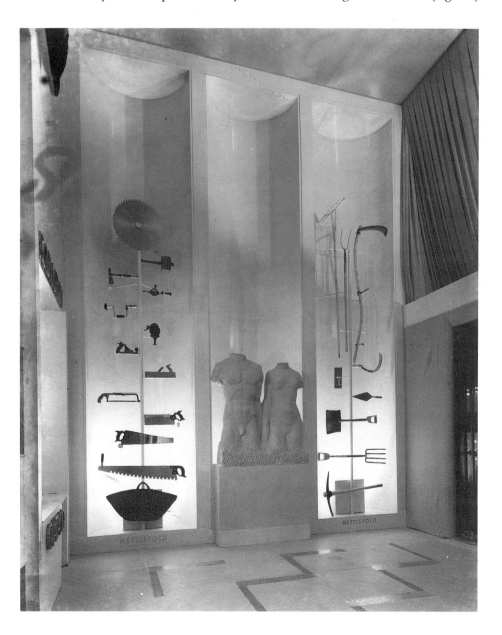

46. *The Exhibition of British Industrial Art and Industry in 1933. Art and Industry symbolised in the vestibule*

47. *Joldwynds, Surrey, designed by Oliver Hill in 1932–33*

at Dartington, a house by Howe and Lescaze which he described as 'probably the most extreme instance in England of the functional type of house associated with the name of Corbusier.' That was followed by a modern flat in Orchard Court and Oswald Milne's Junior School at Dartington. After them came an article on New Thames Bridges and Maufe's Yaffle Hill, which 'exemplifies British Industrial Art'. In the article he said, 'a new synthesis of needs, techniques, and materials has been evolved, capable of replacing the old to which we have clung so long.' And, 'A "synthesis" is what, in our hearts, we are all looking for . . . a formula that will give unity to our lives, and, while preserving beauty, enable our homes to be as simple, and comfortable and well found as are already the car, the ship, the aeroplane. . . . The truth, rather, is that the international technique of functionalism provides the point of departure for national and individual interpretations.' In November Christopher Hussey wrote about Oliver Hill's Midland Hotel at Morecambe, with its relief by Eric Gill, wall paintings by Eric Ravilious and Marion Dorn rugs. The following year he wrote about Oliver Hill's first modern house, Joldwynds (figs. 47, 253-256).

I suspect the year 1933 was something of a watershed for Christopher Hussey. The exhibition grew out of eight years of thought and the fact that it coincided with his accepting the Editorship was bound to lead him to some stock-taking. David Watkin has pointed to Christopher Hussey's growing disenchantment with modern architecture. 'But Hussey's deep understanding of Picturesque theory made him increasingly impatient with advanced Modern Movement architects for their totalitarian insistence on their own style as the only possible style on all occasions, and for their lack of sensitivity to local conditions.'

In December, 1934 he wrote a highly critical review of Raymond McGrath's *Twentieth Century Houses*: 'It will be seen that Mr McGrath's faith in scientific planning and design is uncompromising to the extent

48. *High Cross Hill, one of the buildings at Dartington designed by Lescaze New York*

of fanaticism. When, however, he quits generalities and turns to specific problems and examples, he is on surer ground. The new type of house is still in the experimental stage, and his collection of photographs is useful in suggesting the tendencies at work. A serious criticism of his, and his fellows', view of architecture, however is their complete inability to visualise it in relation to English scenery, or its destructive effect on that scenery. So long as a design is logically, geometrically, and physically complete in itself they are satisfied. But if many such houses were erected, indeed a hundred new cities connected by roads 360 feet wide as envisaged by the author, where would beauty hide herself?'

However the fullest statement of his views dates from just over three years later, when on January 22, 1938, he wrote a review entitled 'Complicated Simplicity' of the New Architecture exhibition by the Mars Group: 'To the already converted, it is easy and natural to approach design as an impersonal, intellectual matter: and they will enjoy the skill with which its abstractions are here set forth. But to the low-brow, the antagonistic, or even the commonplace lover of English scenery who feels vaguely that architecture has something to do with the soil and history, this affair of clicking wheels, diagrammatic silhouettes, and abstract shapes can scarcely fail to be puzzling, if not repellent – which is a great pity . . . The fundamental criticism, however, goes deeper, and concerns the very *credo* of the new architecture. The factor of a building's location and setting, accepted by the traditional designer as a fundamental one controlling the original conception, is omitted here from either the essential or the contributory sections, and only introduced as an incident to the final stage – when the shape, material and, presumably, the plan of the building has already been settled. In relegating the claims of the setting to this tertiary stage, the exhibition faithfully reflects the attitude of the new architects and also the unfriendliness of the new architecture to traditional country landscape. The dogmas of this puritan kind of building must be imposed irrespective of locality, setting, local colour, and tradition. It is essentially an urban-industrial style, well adapted for towns with no particular character, but looking foreign to country landscape. The "Martians" will tell you that they alone approach building in a practical spirit; they are "realists", not "escapists". But why it should be more realistic to sit on the flat roof of a country house, instead of escaping into the garden, I can never make out.'

In the past fifty years *Country Life* has been so closely associated with the preservation movement, particularly of country houses, and developing concepts of preservation and conservation have been so much part of the magazine (increasingly so in the past twenty years), that it is worth looking back to how this particular thread started and how it related to contemporary attitudes. Writers were interested in the restoration of old houses and the proper approach to repairs right from the beginning, and Tipping and Weaver frequently discussed the pros and cons, but protecting monuments and campaigning for their preservation was a comparatively new cause. The National Trust, after all, was only two years old when *Country Life* was founded, and in 1896 it acquired its first modest building, the Clergy House at Alfriston in Sussex. By 1913 it had sixty-two properties, but it was still a very small society with only 700 members. However it had already been recognised by Parliament in 1907, when the first National Trust Act was passed, instituting the principle of inalienability.

Thirty years earlier there had been a great struggle to get any recognition of the need for the protection of ancient monuments by the Government, and the first Ancient Monuments Act had only finally passed in 1882 after years of lobbying led by Sir John Lubbock. After that there was no legislation until the National Trust Act of 1907 and not a single monument was acquired by the state. However in 1908 the Royal Commission on Historical Monuments was set up, but it was conceived in markedly anti-classical terms in that the terminal date for its considerations was set at 1700. (In 1921 it was extended to 1714 but not to 1850 until 1946). In 1911 there was a threat to Tattershall Castle, which was only saved as a result of the last minute intervention of Lord Curzon. He bought back the chimneypieces which had been removed and were about to go abroad, and acquired the castle as well, going on to repair it and give it to the National Trust. That led to the Ancient Monuments Act of 1913.

This very uncertain and unsatisfactory situation is reflected in the pages of *Country Life*, where to start with there was no clearly defined line. On May 6, 1899, for instance, there was an article, 'Destroying a Barn', and on September 17, 1904 there was a plea for help for Barrington Court in Somerset. That was answered three years later when it was acquired by The National Trust largely through Miss J.L. Woodward. The Trust leased it to Colonel Lyle, who repaired it.

The following year on September 30, there was an article on the ruins of East Barsham Manor. That took longer than Barrington Court to evoke a response: restoration did not begin until 1919, and only in 1938 was a start made on making the ruined part habitable again.

In 1914 *Country Life* campaigned against the destruction of 75 Dean Street, Soho, because of its fine interior and painted staircase, and the same year it was involved in the gift of the Hatton Garden Room (fig. 7) to the Victoria and Albert Museum. And on December 12, 1914 the leader was devoted to The Protection of Ancient Churches. But it was only after the First War that *Country Life* became directly involved, with the National Trust, with the Box Hill appeal.

The growing consciousness of how wide the range of historic buildings and their contents was, combined with increased awareness of threats to them as a result of social changes, as well as of economic and planning pressures, was starting to stimulate concern for their preservation; and there again *Country Life* is an interesting mirror.

When Hamilton Palace (figs. 154-157) was described in 1919, the articles were seen as an obituary on one of the most important historic buildings in Scotland, but while, of course, its likely disappearance was regretted, there was no sense in the articles that some official action ought to be taken to prevent it. Indeed throughout the 1920s there are remarkably few pleas for the preservation of houses. It was still very much a private matter. Thus it is interesting to find John Murray writing to Christopher Hussey in May, 1923, asking whether he would write an article for the *Quarterly* some time on the 'decadence of English Country Homes.' 'It is sad to see how one after another they are disappearing, and the same is the case in Scotland. It seems to me that a very interesting article might be made about the passing of these great houses, and the great work which the best of the proprietors has done in the country in years gone by. I have very little doubt that in the long run the wage-earning classes will be heavy sufferers by this; but at present they do not recognise it.' In *Country Life* there are a handful of articles on individual places, on the future of Swakeleys in 1927 and one entitled 'Wanted Preservers. Lymore and Tabley Old Hall' on December 31, 1927; in 1928 there was a two-part and more strongly worded obituary on Dorchester House (figs. 206, 207), London, where considerable efforts had been made to find another user.

At this point it is right to bring in Arthur Oswald (1904-1979), who joined Christopher Hussey in 1928, because, during the forty-one years of his involvement with *Country Life*, he did a great deal to strengthen the scholarly aspect of the articles on country houses that was to become increasingly important in the way *Country Life* was regarded, not least by those concerned with issues and policies of preservation. A gentle, shy, retiring man, Arthur Oswald was not really suited to the particular combination of pressures at *Country Life*, a way of writing that demands time and leisure and yet has to be produced on the day, and often the day before, because of changes in press dates. By nature he was an academic, who should have enjoyed the degree of protection provided by membership of a college, and, indeed, having taught for two years before he came to *Country Life*, his hope and intention had been to combine university teaching with *Country Life* work as a secondary activity.

By inclination he was really a mediaevalist, with a particular love of church architecture, and he did a great deal of pioneer research on mediaeval masons that was of use to John Harvey when he was compiling his dictionary of mediaeval architects. However, in his early years on the magazine, he was imposed on by Hudson, having to produce many articles that did not really interest him, and it was only gradually that his particular kind of careful documentary research and physical examination of buildings came to have a bearing on the overall standard of *Country Life*. In 1933 he produced his *Country Houses of Kent*, and two years later his *Country Houses of Dorset*, which he revised in 1959. Certainly in later years he spent much longer on the preparation of his articles than his colleagues, and while that meant a tendency to draw them out from one to two and two to three parts, his accounts of buildings have not only stood the test of time, but his researches contributed a great deal to the work of other scholars. Almost inevitably he was overshadowed by Christopher Hussey, who was not only older and already established but was also a much more outgoing personality, but certainly when he returned to the office after service in the Navy during the Second War he made a distinctive contribution to *Country Life*, so that just by looking at the illustrations one knew it was an 'Arthur' house or town that was being described.

In 1930 there is a distinct change in the character of the leaders in *Country Life*, which were generally written by Christopher Hussey, Bernard Darwin or Edmund Barber, who decided between themselves about the theme for that week. About mid-day Barber used to have to slip out of the office to make a telephone call to his mother – so he said – but he apparently wrote excellent leaders when he had had plenty to drink. However those on architecture, preservation and planning must have been written by Christopher Hussey. On January 25, 1930, there was a particularly arresting one entitled 'The National Heritage', which only needs a few names changing to make it relevant today. It deserves publication as a whole, but one extract must suffice: 'That our great country houses, with their treasures of art, their wide-spreading parks and delightful gardens have now come to be considered as national and not merely personal heritages we owe to the generosity and practical public spirit of the landowners of today. But in the present financial circumstances such generosity cannot be extended indefinitely, and we may well ask whether the Government will not do something practical to prevent the constant breaking up of beautiful properties into ugly building estates and the dispersal abroad of well-nigh priceless collections. The state has already exempted from death duties works of art of public interest. Why should it not extend this principle to parks and woods and open spaces such as those of Goodwood, which, though privately owned, are always open for public enjoyment, and to houses such as Knole, which are in reality national treasure houses of beautiful things? . . . '

That leader was written four years before Lord Lothian's speech to the National Trust, and it marks a new and much more positive approach to preservation issues. Two years later, for instance, there was an article on Appuldurcombe and a leader criticising the proposal to demolish Carlton House Terrace, which was followed up by a fiery diatribe by Robert Byron.

In the summer of 1935 Lord Lothian made a second speech about country houses to the British Antique Dealers Association, which prompted *Country Life* to devote its leader to 'The Future of Country Houses': 'Death duties imposed in 1904, with the maximum rate of eight per cent, have since 1930 risen to a maximum rate of fifty per cent, and the full effect of the tax has not as yet been felt. "Looking at the picture," Lord Lothian said last year, "I do not think it is an exaggeration to say that within a generation hardly one of these historic houses, save perhaps a few in the neighbourhood of London, will be lived in by the families who created them . . ." It seems obvious that our traditional system of land tenure and agriculture cannot survive under this penal code of taxation unless those who are compelled to endure it are given some substantial relief, and the services, which they perform to the nation, are to some extent at least recognised . . .'

In the same year, when the future of Bramshill (figs. 265, 266, 267) was uncertain, Christopher Hussey wrote an impassioned article on August 17 based on attitudes in tune with those leaders.

At the end of that year, the leader was again devoted to country houses: to 'Trust Funds for Country Houses', which would be tax free for the maintenance of country houses of approved architectural importance, to which the public has regular access. The case was carefully argued, and only the costs seem incredible today: it was felt that a tax-free income of £830 a year would look after a house in a park of three-hundred acres, with ten acres of gardens and forty rooms: that would be the wages for two men for the park at £200, five gardeners at £550 and £80 for the house.

In 1936, as we have seen, the National Trust appointed its Country Houses Commmittee, which soon in its turn appointed a sub-committee to draw up a list of two hundred houses of undoubted merit. Christopher Hussey was, not surprisingly, chosen to be one of the number. The following year the first major offer, Stourhead, was made to the Trust under the new scheme, and although it did not go through until 1946, it is interesting to find in 1938 an article by Christopher Hussey on the landscape. He starts by quoting Sir Richard Colt Hoare: 'We ought to consider ourselves as existing not solely for ourselves; to bear in mind *non sibi sed posteris*. It was this superb, forward looking confidence of the late Georgian squires that gave us our English landscape, by a process of which Stourhead is an outstanding, if a concentrated product; our English landscape that, in this full tide of democracy, we are so hopelessly failing to preserve, or to realise as something created and therefore easily destructible.'

Reading that article it quickly comes to mind that Christopher Hussey was the grandson of just such a late Georgian squire, and he himself was the author of one of the most influential books on landscape that was inspired by what his grandfather had done.

The Stourhead article appeared shortly after his review of the MARS group exhibition and it explains why he himself was in the process of changing direction. He saw the leaders of the Modern Movement were promoting an architecture that was alien to and destructive of the English tradition and the English landscape.

PART TWO

The English Interior
Through the Eyes of
Country Life

49. Sledmere, Yorkshire. The south hall in 1897

Sledmere

YORKSHIRE

These were the first interiors to be published in *Country Life*, on March 6, 1897. They were included in an article on the house that appears almost as an afterthought to two on the Sledmere Stud, and they were taken by W.A. Rouch, a well-known blood stock photographer (and are reproduced from copy negatives). The articles on the stud were regarded as a 'scoop', *Country Life* being 'the first journal to whom the privilege of producing photographic portraits of the inmates of this world-renowned stud has been accorded'. The house itself was described as 'a fine old Grecian building,' and typically the emphasis was on its ancient history, 'since it was rebuilt by Sir Christopher Sykes in 1760 [in fact it was begun in 1784 and completed in the 1790s], on the site of the old Manor, which dated back to the year 1430.'

Sadly, the two photographs were to prove valuable as a record: in 1911 Sledmere was gutted by fire, and they were part of the evidence available to Walter Brierley when he came to reconstruct it, a commission illustrated on October 18, 1918 (figs. 151, 152). Brierley's principal alteration to the main house was to open up the original South Hall, Inner Hall and Staircase Hall to form a spectacular space. Rouch's record of the South Hall, with its curved inner wall and niches containing stoves, gives an idea of the original balance of the rooms while showing how carefully Brierley restored the details of the plasterwork.

The Library is seen in a state of contrived disorder that seems to have been dear to late Victorians and soon was to be considered unsuitable. Presumably the generation of Sir Tatton Sykes, the 5th baronet, in whose time the photograph was taken, found the great vaulted gallery designed as a library by the first Sir Christopher too architectural and uncomfortable in mood as the main sitting room of the house, so they broke it up through the arrangement of the furniture. Perhaps only the late Sir Richard and Lady Sykes fully enjoyed using it in the years after the Second War, when Sledmere could have been the setting for a novel by Evelyn Waugh. In 1978 one of their sons, Christopher Simon Sykes, compiled a vivid pictorial record of the house and his family in *The Visitors' Book*.

Hatfield House

HERTFORDSHIRE

Since the early nineteenth century Hatfield has been regarded as the archetypal great country house, both in terms of its architecture and of the history of the Cecil family. In the late eighteenth century, however, the original Jacobean processional route from the Great Hall, up the stairs to this Great Room of State and on to the State Bedroom was broken up, and this room became the principal drawing room of the house. Of its original decoration the chimney-piece and overmantel incorporating the statue of King James I is the main survivor, and the room is now a synthesis of dates and changing interpretations by a succession of generations, including the present Marquess and Marchioness of Salisbury. This photograph records it in the time of the 3rd Marquess, Queen Victoria's Prime Minister (and the last to sit in

50. (Opposite) *Sir Christopher Sykes's classical library in Victorian disguise*

51. (Below) *The King James Drawing Room. The Victorian embellishments have been swept away*

the House of Lords), who is now the dominant historical personality in the house. He belonged to a generation who believed, or pretended to believe, that 'Taste' and an interest in visual matters was improper, and Lord David Cecil in *The Cecils of Hatfield House* (1973) quotes him saying to a prospective daughter-in-law, 'Welcome to Hatfield, its other name is Gaza, the capital of Philistia.' That, however, did not prevent him doing a good deal to the house, including being the first to instal electric light in an old house, and inserting in this room in 1889/90 the high panelled and painted dado and the vertical panels of painted decoration flanking the full length portraits seen here. The Cecils have never produced a collector of pictures, so it has always been a problem how to clothe the walls of this room in a suitable fashion, and the 3rd Marquess's combination of full-length portraits and panelling was an ingenious one. Certainly it was much admired by John Leyland, who described it as being 'gorgeous in its adornments of marble, gold and colour . . . ' in his articles of May 8 and 15, 1897. However the photograph (reproduced from a copy negative) taken by H.N. King, evidently a general commercial photographer rather than an architectural specialist, was not of high quality, and, although the only interior illustrated, it was reproduced quite small.

Sutton Place
SURREY

Since *Country Life* has been so closely involved with architectural preservation, it is interesting to find that as early as 1898 it was concerned with approaches to restoration and repair. In the article published on December 31 on Sutton Place, which at that time was rented from the Salvins by Mr Lawrence Harrison, the anonymous author wrote: '*Country Life* has depicted several homes rescued from decay – some even from oblivion. In days of rural depression such places should be the joy of English men.' That joy was conceived in high flown but rather vague terms: 'We are in the days when barbican and frowning battlement had fallen before the more peaceful influence of a later time . . . ' No attempt was made to investigate its building in the reign of Henry VIII or discuss the celebrated Italianate terracotta decoration of its elevations.

The photograph was evidently taken by Charles Latham, the brilliant architectural photographer who established the style of *Country Life* illustration of houses and gardens; but for some reason all the interiors were reproduced smaller than the exteriors.

The Harrisons, who had lived in the house for a number of years and were responsible in 1878 for the formation of the Long Gallery in its present form, gave it up in 1900. Since then it has belonged to a succession of very rich owners, so that it has lost much of the romantic patina apparent at the end of the last century.

52. (Below) *The long gallery*

53. (Opposite) *A view into the hall*

Munstead Wood

Surrey

This was a key house in the success of Edwin Lutyens, not only in terms of its quality but also of his reputation and his future. His client, friend and promoter, Gertrude Jekyll, had bought the site in 1882 and begun the garden, but only after her mother's death in 1895 did she feel free to build herself a house there. Naturally she turned to Lutyens, whom she had first met in 1889 when he was twenty. Building was carried out in 1896-97, and immediately the house aroused the interest of friends and neighbours. The young Robert Lorimer, for instance, who went there as soon as she moved in, wrote to R.S. Dods in Australia: 'Who do you think did this for her, a young chap called Lutyens, twenty-seven he is, and I've heard him described by the Schultz school as a "society" architect. Miss J. has pretty well run him.'

Harold Falkener, the architect, described how 'one was ushered in through a stone and oak hall and corridor, with glints of bright brasswork, old oak and blue china. One found oneself in the principal living room of the house – a large, hall-like room with plenty of comfortable chairs, tables littered with books, furniture in well-polished wood and lacquer, and generally a log fire in an enormous stone-hooded ingle.' That is amplified by the author of the *Country Life* article on December 8, 1900, who wrote: 'Inside, again, there is little which flashes upon the visitor or astonishes him; all is beautifully plain and massive. At first he feels everything is exactly as it should be. It is only little by little that he realises the details that produce the feeling – the width of the hall, with its huge beams still bearing the adze marks, the fine proportions of the fireplace with its glowing fire of oaken billets, the noble array of pewter in the dining room, the massive simplicity of the staircase, the light and space of the gallery with its immemorial beams . . .' (seen here in photographs from copy negatives.)

Edward Hudson was presumably first taken to see the house when he wanted to persuade Gertrude Jekyll to write about gardening for *Country Life*. She promptly introduced him to Lutyens, with the immediate result that Hudson asked him to design The Deanery Garden at Sonning (figs. 72, 73).

54. (Below) *The hall or sitting room.*

55. (Opposite above) *The Oak Gallery*

56. (Opposite below) *Gerrude Jekyll's work room*

Haddon Hall

DERBYSHIRE

'The transcendental delight of the home of the Vernons lies in its happy union of history and poetry with rare beauty of architecture and the external charms of the old garden, and a beautiful neighbouring land. Where else can we receive such impressions of ancient greatness touched with the witchery of bygone romance?' These sentences do not come from Henry James, who had been deeply impressed by Haddon in the early 1870s, but from the long article – it ran to eleven pages with illustrations on two more – published in *Country Life* on June 1, 1901.

At that time Haddon was seldom occupied by the 8th Duke of Rutland, but his son, Lord Granby, who was born in 1885 and became 9th Duke in 1925, fell in love with the place as a boy. Many years later one of his sisters, Lady Violet Benson, described how he used to save his pocket money while away at school, sending it to her so that she could go with her governess to hunt for old oak furniture for the Hall in farm houses round about. His enthusiasm could have been fired by his mother, Violet, Duchess of Rutland, a talented artist and a leading figure in the circle of the Souls. In 1912, when he was twenty-six, Lord Granby decided to embark on Haddon's repair and make it his home, a task that took him many years. The view into the chapel shows the still whitewashed walls rather than the late fifteenth century grisaille wall painting that he and Professor Tristram discovered later. The photograph of the Great Bay in the Long Gallery reveals the technical difficulty of taking such photographs: the part of the negative showing the glazing is so retouched that a print from it looks almost like a water colour.

57. *The great bay in the long gallery*

58. (Opposite) *The entrance to the chapel*

Old Place, Lindfield

Sussex

Surprisingly this was one of the favourite places in the early years of *Country Life*, with no less than three articles on the house and garden, on October 6 1900, July 20 1901 and September 21 1907. The house was the creation of C.A. Kempe, a designer of stained glass who also worked as a decorator of houses, and died in April, 1907. The first article was devoted to the exterior of the house and the garden – 'whatever is new here is own brother to the old' – and the second on the house, in 1901, by C.J. Cornish, was entitled *Art Within and Without*. In it he wrote that Mr Kempe 'has for more than twenty years devoted his trained hand and intellect to its building and decoration. The result represents, probably, the highest development of contemporary taste and skill in artistic design, subordinated to mod-

ern needs and requirements.' The strongly painterly approach, the eclectic collecting of continental as well as English objects and the links between past and present are all apparent in the description of the dining room: 'The ancient hangings on the walls of this fine room are of a green tint, against which large silver sconces shine, and foliage tapestry scarcely distinguishable from ancient examples, but recently woven on the looms of France, testifies to the skill of the modern weaver when working under the educating influences of the student in ancient art.' The elaborate writing is in tune with the slightly heavy and overdone character of the rooms that is so different in mood from Munstead (fig. 7) and The Deanery Garden (fig. 73).

59. (Below) *The great parlour*

60. (Opposite above) *The dining room*

61. (Opposite below) *The dial room*

Orchards

Surrey

'I saw the beautiful *Country Life* photos of Orchards which will come out in CL soon & Bumps [Gertrude Jekyll] is writing the description.' So Lutyens wrote excitedly to his wife on August 11, 1901. The article, in fact, appeared on August 31, and, what was unusual at that stage, was signed by the author. Miss Jekyll had more to say about the garden than the interior, but the choice of subjects for illustration, the Dining Room (shown here in a print from a copy negative), the Oak Passage on the first floor and stairs leading to Mrs Chance's studio, was followed in many later articles on Lutyens' houses. Only in the last sentence, however, did she mention Lutyens' name as the architect. It was particularly appropriate that Edward Hudson asked her to write it, because it was through her that Lutyens had received the commission in 1897. Mr and Mrs William Chance (he succeeded to the baronetcy in 1902) had intended that Halsey Ricardo should design their new house – indeed his design was published in *The Architectural Review* – but, as a result of calling on Miss Jekyll in the spring of 1897 and seeing her new house, they decided to go to Lutyens instead. Orchards was one of the houses admired by Muthesius, and it was illustrated in *Das Englische Haus* in 1904.

62. *Architectural dressers in the dining room*

Drakelowe Hall

DERBYSHIRE

Today the now vanished house at Drakelowe on the Derbyshire-Staffordshire border near Burton-on-Trent immediately calls to mind this magical room, of which only one wall was saved when the house was demolished in about 1934, and was re-erected in the Victoria and Albert Museum. In the article of March 22, 1902, the main emphasis was on the garden and on the long history of the Gresleys; the only interior illustrated (shown here in a print from a copy negative) was this room commissioned by Sir Nigel Gresley, the seventh baronet. 'The very remarkable painted dining-room, which belongs, of course, to much later times, and yet is not in accord with the taste of these days,' wrote the author. 'Few such rooms exist, but they were not uncommon in the reigns of Queen Anne and the Georges.' It was a singular fancy that made men wish, while in their houses, to seem to be out of doors.' Although described at some length, no date was given nor was there any mention that it was painted by Paul Sandby, even though it was signed and dated. When the house was described again, in March 16, 1907, the same photograph was used, together with other interiors, and then the room was attributed to Paul Sandby. Even so it was still not admired: 'The depraved taste of the late eighteenth century turned the large dining room into a panorama of the Peak Country.'

63. *The painted dining room by Paul Sandby*

Wilton House

WILTSHIRE

It was natural that Wilton appeared fairly early in the series of Country Homes, on April 12, 1902, because it has always been one of the most celebrated houses in England. Moreover, like many great houses it has been regularly open to visitors, with a series of guidebooks dating back to 1731. Also it inspired possibly the earliest country house caricature: Rowlandson's drawing of being shown this room, which was done for his *Tour in a Post Chaise*, probably in 1784. As the author wrote in *English Homes* I, 'Its associations are interwoven with the lives of the famous, it is in itself a wonderful architectural creation, its noble apart-

ments contain many masterpieces of great sculptors and painters, and it is surrounded by gardens surpassingly beautiful.' The response was essentially romantic, and, although the broad outlines of the history of the house were well understood, perhaps because they had never been forgotten, there was little or no attempt to dig deeply into the details of its development. And naturally no comment on the crowded appearance of the rooms (seen here in a print from a copy negative). How the latter developed has been little studied, and more research needs to be done on early photographs of interiors. Surprisingly the first full account of Wilton did not appear in *Country Life* until Christopher Hussey wrote a long series of articles in 1963 to mark its restoration and rearrangement by the late Earl of Pembroke, who did so much to unearth its history.

64. *The Double Cube room in Edwardian confusion*

65. (Opposite) *Lord Zouche's armour in the Baron's Hall at Parham*

Parham Park

SUSSEX

The Hall at Parham (shown here in a print from a copy negative) is an admirable illustration of changing romantic taste in England over the past one hundred and fifty years, because its appearance is recorded in almost every generation since Nash published his view in *Mansions of England in the Olden Time*. There are early photographs in Mark Girouard's *The Return to Camelot*, and *Country Life* took up the story on April 19, 1902, returning there in 1951 (fig. 10) and 1985. In 1902 it was the seat of the 15th Lord Zouche, who had succeeded his remarkable father in 1873. Born in 1810 and so a generation younger than Lord Byron and William Bankes of Kingston Lacy, the 14th Baron shared their taste for the Romantic and

Exotic as can be seen not only in his book *Monasteries of the Levant* (1844) and Ian Fraser's recent biography *The Heir of Parham*, but also in his collection of arms and armour, much of which he collected in the Middle East. However, after many years of frustrating waiting to inherit, he had only a short period in complete control at Parham, succeeding his mother in 1870 and dying three years later. The author of the 1902 article called him 'a nobleman of fine taste, who richly stored his house with precious things. He made a great collection of early armour, and the display at Parham was almost unrivalled, while the gold and silver plate and ivory carvings were very beautiful, and the library was rich in ancient manuscripts.' In 1922 the house was acquired by the Hon. Clive and Mrs Pearson who carried out a sensitive restoration over the next forty-three years and filled the house with a fascinating collection of historical portraits, furniture and textiles.

Sandringham

Norfolk

It was a tribute to the rapid growth of *Country Life*'s reputation that it was permitted to send a photographer to Sandringham in 1902 and take a series of pictures, twenty of which were illustrated in an article of fourteen pages on June 7. The text, while making no mention of the history of the 7,000 acre estate bought by the Prince of Wales shortly before his marriage in 1863, out of the capital skilfully built up for him during his minority by his father, or of the house largely rebuilt in 1870 to the

66. (Opposite) *Queen Alexandra's portrait in the drawing room*

67. (Below) *The billiards room*

design of an obscure architect, A.J. Humbert, is remarkably unfulsome and straightforward: 'Of some owners of great estates and huge houses it has been said, often and but too truly, that they have many palaces but no home; but that most certainly cannot be said of the King and Queen, who have made Sandringham and Marlborough House, both of them, into real homes'. 'Of mere splendour there is not much, but of substantial comfort a good deal.' He responded to the many mementoes of the royal couple's travels to be seen everywhere, the feeling of sunlight in the house and the profusion of flowers and plants. 'In a word Sandringham is not grand; it is not meant so to be; but it is essentially and emphatically bright and comfortable.' Here, as Sir Philip Magnus explained in his life of Edward VII, he used to come in time for his birthday in early November and stay on until the end of February, enjoying the shooting: 'Guests noticed that he enjoyed practical jokes, that he made a point of arranging personally such details

as bedroom allocations and seating at meals.' Moreover he and the Princess were popular in the neighbourhood, because 'They gave County, farmers' and servants' balls at regular intervals, and delighted labourers who earned extra money by serving as beaters on shooting days.' The author explained that 'a better tract of land for keeping together a great head of game and for showing it in a sportsmanlike fashion it would be impossible to conceive,' and commented on a custom apparently copied from Lord Leicester's practice at Holkham: 'guests and visitors to Sandringham were early given to understand that at Sandringham, Sandringham time was kept. If they were asked to assemble at a given rendezvous for shooting at ten, that really meant – and still means – half-past nine; and so you get half an hour more daylight.' Of the portrait of the Queen, the author wrote: 'Mr Hughes is no Gainsborough, but in the production of what may be called "Pleasant family likenesses," he is without rival; and this particular portrait of Queen Alexandra is one of

the most successful that he has ever done.' Of the Goya tapestries in the dining room he wrote: 'their colouring was originally somewhat crude . . . [but] they had mellowed not a little' and ' . . . In a few years they will be better still.' Also, 'Somehow or other there seem to be more long passages or corridors in Sandringham than in most houses, except Osborne. . . . The billiard room itself is quite one of the brightest rooms in the house, and just what a billiard room should be. All the pictures are sketches by John Leech, and they are all familiar friends – one cannot have too much of John Leech.'

68. (Opposite) *The saloon. The entrance hall and principal living room are combined here*

69. (Below) *The King's library*

Hewell Grange

WORCESTERSHIRE

Splendid as it was when filled with works of art and set in elaborate Old English gardens that went with its gables and mullioned windows, there must have always been a certain dryness and lack of warmth about it. Mark Girouard has written of how one can see there 'the first freezing of the smile on the face of the country house.' Commissioned in 1884 by Lord Windsor, then aged twenty-six and recently married, it was designed by Bodley and Garner (whose names are not mentioned in the article in *Country Life* on December 6, 1902). Replacing what must have then seemed a rather dull Midland Baroque house, externally it was in the picturesque style of 'Charles or James', as the author of the article vaguely described it. Within however, 'we are confronted with splendid work that could be at home in some palace of Italy,' with its hall as its main feature: 'the ruling idea in the designing of this great and imposing Hall was majesty in character and richness in materials and handicraft. Marbles and travertine, the products of the most celebrated quarries, splendid woodwork, and the best that the craftsmen in plaster could accomplish, nothing was spared that could beautify the interior.' Lord Windsor – he was later created Earl of Plymouth – and his wife were the opposite of philistine aristocrats: he was not only a collector of Italian pictures but the leading preserver of the Crystal Palace, the man largely responsible for the laying out of the Mall and also the second chairman of the National Trust. Lady Windsor, who was painted by Burne Jones, was a Soul. Their conception of Hewell was soon to prove an anachronism, for only two years after it was completed, death duties were introduced.

70 and 71. (Below and opposite) *The great hall and its galleries*

The Deanery Garden, Sonning

BERKSHIRE

This was the first commission that Edward Hudson, the founder of *Country Life*, gave to Edwin Lutyens, in 1899. Perhaps surprisingly he allowed it to be published in *The Architectural Review* in 1902 before *Country Life* (May 9, 1903), where it appeared in a series of articles rather archly entitled *Houses for People with Hobbies*. Also it was the only new house included in the first volume of Latham's *In English Homes*. In neither article is there mention of Hudson's name, and the whole tone of the *Country Life* article is underplayed, seeing it first as the house of a man with a hobby, rose growing and wall gardening; second, to show what could be accomplished in a very short space of time; and third as being 'as characteristic a specimen of the style of Mr E.L. Lutyens as is extant at the moment.'

It surely says a great deal about Hudson's elusive personality that he was able to stimulate Lutyens to produce what proved to be one of his masterpieces. Not only was it a brilliant piece of architecture that develops several of the ideas seen at Munstead, but the interior suggests a sensitive, light touch in its furnishing and arrangement which makes an interesting comparison with the heavier feeling of Old Place at Lingfield (figs. 59, 60, 61) or Tipping's contemporary Oak Room at Mathern Palace (fig. 117). As the author said, 'There is much oak-work and panelling in the hall, and old pewter and brass and a hundred things are there to delight the collector.' Hudson must have been amused when, after his time, the house was advertised for sale in *Country Life* in 1906 by Hamptons, who described 'this choice little place' as a 'very beautiful Elizabethan House perfectly true in character and detail.'

72. (Opposite) *The hall from the entrance*

73. (Below) *The gallery. It was partly inspired by the gallery at Munstead seen in Fig 55*

Groombridge Place
KENT

From the beginning *Country Life* was catholic, or eclectic, in its choice of houses: it had to give readers variety, of scale, style and location. So it was part of its secret to move from the splendours of Hewell to the essential domesticity of Caroline Groombridge; and again the gardens were described before the interior, which was illustrated on September 19, 1903. The house was built about 1660 by Philip Packer, a friend of John Evelyn from student days at the Middle Temple; and, although it passed through several different ownerships, it has always retained the Packer portraits. In 1903, when it belonged to the Misses Saint, it represented one kind of perfect house, its internal features presenting 'that domestic aspect which should be found in all houses that do not partake of the character of palaces.'

Also it was completely unspoiled: 'There is no intrusion of the twentieth century here. The lighting is by candles.' Of the drawing room the author wrote: 'The ceiling is ... peculiarly enriched in its plasterwork, which represents fruit and foliage. There are grand old mirrors, Chippendale chairs, others of older type, portraits of the Packers and an especially beautiful old crystal chandelier for its plenishings.' In 1919, on the death of the last Miss Saint, the house was bought by Mr H.S. Mountain, who furnished it with great sensitivity round the Packer portraits that still remain here.

74. A synthesis of periods in the drawing room

Belton House

LINCOLNSHIRE

Belton was so greatly admired in the opening years of this century that it was the first house in the first volume of *In English Homes*, published in 1904. It was chosen for that prominent position, because it 'bears upon its face all the characteristics of the great architect who designed it, as his mind was expressed in his domestic creations. That architect was Sir Christopher Wren.' By that time Wren was seen not only as the hero of English architecture but as a great inspiration to contemporaries – and the choice of Belton to open that book parallels Hudson's commission to Lutyens to design the *Country Life* building in a Wrenaissance style.

There was another parallel between past and present in the way the article, published on October 31, 1903, was presented. Surprisingly it did not include any exteriors, but concentrated entirely on the carvings by Grinling Gibbons, whose work was much admired and sought after. The author wrote: 'There are no finer examples of the work of the great woodcarver in England, and his masterpieces at Belton have had the advantage of being subjected to restoration by that eminent artist, who followed so much in his footsteps, the late W.G. Rogers.'

75. One of the overmantels in the hall, then attributed to Grinling Gibbons

Ockwells

BERKSHIRE

Fashions in old houses swing rather more than might be expected, and in the 1980s Ockwells perhaps does not arouse quite such general enthusiasm as it did eighty or ninety years ago. Built by Sir John Norreys between 1446 and 1466, it is described by Sir Nikolaus Pevsner as 'the most refined and the most sophisticated timber-framed mansion in England. It is true its perfection is partly due to the twentieth century restoration by Fairfax Wade.' He worked for Edward Barry, who rescued it from being a farm house. In the view of some, rather too much was done, and the textures are a little dead, but there is no doubt about the enthusiasm of the writer of the article on April 2, 1904: 'Few people realise what it was to raise in those days so glorious a house. There was something in the operation analagous to the building of a ship – the same need for seasoned oak, the same labour with saw and adze, the same pegging of joint and tenon, and so the structure rose complete and solid. There was super-added the fine craft of the carver, the loving labour of the man who fashioned the cusped window frames, the magnificent barge boards, and the finials. Then came the glass-stainer, with his splendid blazonry, to flood the rooms with colour, and the tapestry, often from distant looms, and the ladies in their bower working at fair embroideries for the adornment of the abode.' Given that imaginative, poetic approach, it is small wonder that the perfection is partly twentieth century.

76. (Below) *The great hall*

77. (Opposite above left) *The buttery hatch*

78. (Opposite above right) *The recess in the great hall*

79. (Opposite below left) *The screens passage*

80. (Opposite below right) *The south passage*

Kingston Lacy

DORSET

Country Life has always been run economically, and authors who ask a photographer to take more photographs than are likely to be used are frowned on: plans were so carefully made that often everything was published. Occasionally, however, a run through the negatives for a house reveals an unpublished illustration of interest. For instance, when the article on Kingston Lacy appeared on April 16, 1904, the view of the library was included, but not that of the drawing room, which had been only recently refurnished by Mrs R.W. Bankes. Born Henrietta Jane Fraser, she had married R.W. Bankes in 1897, and the following year she hung the drawing room with rose coloured damask and furnished it in an up-to-date eighteenth-century revival style to complement the portraits, so making up

for what one of her predecessors had taken away. Her husband died in 1904, leaving a son aged two, and it was the latter who left Kingston Lacy together with its pictures to the National Trust in 1982. The photograph of the drawing room was invaluable to the Trust when it came to arrange the room in 1986, and the library still looks very much as it did, except that the out-of-scale painting by Guido Reni has been taken down from the ceiling. It was one of the pictures acquired by William Bankes (1786–1855), a friend of Byron, who spent the years 1812–1820 travelling in Spain, the Middle East and Italy and formed the marvellous collection of pictures that remains in the house. Before he fled abroad in 1841, he planned to place Tintoretto's *Apollo and the Muses* on the library ceiling, but he did not do so, and the Reni was put up later, and not by him.

81. (Below) *Eighteenth-century revival in the drawing room*

82. (Opposite) *Lely portraits in the library*

Clouds
WILTSHIRE

This was one of the centres of the circle of the Souls, romantic and artistic, domestic and comfortable. Commissioned from Philip Webb in 1876 by the Hon. Percy Wyndham, building began in 1881 and was finished in 1886. In 1889 the house was burned, but then rebuilt within the next three years. By November 19, 1904, when Wilfrid Scawen Blunt, who was a first cousin of Percy Wyndham and an amateur architect, wrote about it in *Country Life*, Philip Webb had retired from practice. But as Blunt wrote: 'His name is one reverenced by the craft and worshipped by not a few of the best architects of the rising generation.'

Interestingly enough those remarks are echoed in one of Lutyens' few contributions to *Country Life*, an article on the work of Webb published on May 8, 1915 to mark his death: 'It must have been in 1891 that I first saw an example of Philip Webb's work, and I remember exclaiming, That's good; I wonder who the young man is?'

Of the decoration and furnishing of the house Blunt wrote: The living-rooms are models of dignified simplicity, a little plain may be, according to our ideas of modern ornament, but of that exact proportion which is in itself the greatest and purest pleasure to the eye a room can give. There are very few curtains, and those chiefly Morris tapestries of various hues, the hangings in the drawing-room being simply white. There is no elaboration either of design or contrast, and the Morris carpets are the only luxury of colour.' It is fascinating to be able to compare his reaction with that of Lady Paget, writing from Hewell in 1895: 'I returned from white and blue Clouds, charming in its way, to this house blazing with gorgeous Italian colour.'

83. *The great hall*

84. (Opposite above) *The drawing room*

85. (Opposite below) *The morning room*

86. *The long gallery at Sudbury. Like the library at Sledmere and the gallery at Hatfield, it became an extended living room during the nineteenth century.*

Sudbury Hall

Derbyshire

The Gallery at Sudbury, completed by George Vernon in the 1670s, is a marvellous room: it runs the full length of the garden front, with its great windows looking south over the garden and lake; overhead are a succession of richly framed circles and ovals with garlands of fruit and flowers modelled by Bradbury and Pettifer, and on the walls hang a series of vivid portraits of George Vernon's family by Michael Wright. Some time in the mid nineteenth century the gallery was fitted out with deal bookcases to take the library formed by the 5th Lord Vernon, as can be seen in this photograph included in the article of April 8, 1905. In 1922 when the 9th Lord Vernon returned to live in the house, some redecoration and re-arranging was done, as can be seen when the house was next described in *Country Life*, in 1935 (fig. 261).

Holland House

London

'The omnibuses . . . pass the walls of a park, into which the people of London, which has broken into the Royal parks one by one, has not yet gained entry. The crests upon the gates and lodges are those of a family . . . ' So wrote the author of the article on the house published on June 17, 1905. What is remarkable is that Holland House remained the home of a family until its destruction in the Second World War. It had an outstandingly rich history: originally built for Sir Walter Cope about 1606-1607, its principal interior was the Gilt Room, on the first floor in the centre of the main front. The painting of its panelling was probably done about 1625 for Henry Rich, 1st Earl of Holland, who had a hand in the decoration of Ham House.

87. *The Gilt Room at Holland House. It was perhaps the richest surviving example of the taste in decoration of the court of Charles I*

Earlshall
FIFE

Earlshall was the first restoration-cum-recreation carried out by Robert Lorimer, who worked not only on the fabric of the house but on its furnishing and the layout of the garden. Repairs began as soon as R.W.R. Mackenzie acquired it as a semi-ruin in 1891. Lorimer had known the place when young, because it is only a few miles from Kellie Castle, which his father first leased as a summer house in 1878. He, however, was trained in the South, in Bodley's office, and he knew both Lutyens and Gertrude Jekyll; and, as Muthesius pointed out in 1904, it was he who took back to Scotland the English appreciation of vernacular building and applied it to the Scottish tradition.

Lorimer had great historical sense as well as a feeling for materials, and it is interesting to find him copying the Falkland screen illustrated by MacGibbon and Ross, in *The Castellated and Domestic Architecture of Scotland* (1887-1892), a feature that Tipping also, and with less justification, used at Brinsop Court (fig. 139). In his memorial book about Lorimer in 1931, Christopher Hussey said: 'If he had not had this opportunity to make a name for himself, while still in his twenties, as a brilliant and sympathetic restorer of Scottish buildings, the whole trend of his development might have been different, or at least his revitalising influence on Scottish tradition would have been delayed.'

The article on Earlshall, which was published on July 1, 1905, does not mention Lorimer's name, and Peter Savage, in his book on Lorimer, says that it was written by Lawrence Weaver. That would make it his earliest identified contribution to *Country Life* as well as the first article in the magazine on Lorimer, but there is no clue as to how it came about. It is conceivable that both the subject and the author was suggested to Edward Hudson by Gertrude Jekyll.

Weaver's sympathy for Lorimer's work is apparent in his description of the restoration of the painted decoration in the Gallery: 'The painting was all on timber, which the rain through the roof had made too rotten for a nail to stay in, and much had already fallen. Piece by piece the surface was sliced away, and glued like veneer to sound wood, which could then be secured as in former time to the upper couples of the roof. This achieved, the painting, still clearly to be seen, was slowly brought back to its original colours by distemper.'

88. *The hall with Lorimer's screen copied from Falkland Palace*

89. (Opposite above) *The seventeenth-century painted gallery*

90. (Opposite below) *An old Scottish kitchen. It shows some of the earliest furniture designed by Lorimer in one of the cottages*

91. (Above) *Elizabethan decoration in the drawing room*

92. (Right) *The Lewis Wyatt dining room. In the late 1970s this room was restored partly on the basis of this photograph*

Lyme Park

CHESHIRE

Lyme has a rare strength that arises partly from the way that the great quadrangular house sits high up in its park above Stockport, with the moorland rising behind it, and partly from the long history of the Leghs, descendents of the first Sir Piers who was granted the property by Richard II in recognition of his father-in-law's service at Crecy. In 1892 they were granted the more prosaic-sounding barony of Newton in Lancashire, and in 1898 the house passed to the 2nd Baron and his wife, a Bromley-Davenport from Capesthorne. Lady Newton had immense pride and interest in the history of the family and wrote two excellent books based on the papers, *The House of Lyme* (1917) and *Lyme Letters* (1925). Moreover Lyme in their generation inspired one of the best country house books, a lightly disguised account of an Edwardian Christmas called *Treasure on Earth* written by their youngest daughter, Phyllis Sandeman (first published in 1952 and reissued in 1971).

Writing elsewhere Phyllis Sandeman recalled, 'Soon after taking up residence at Lyme, my mother began on her "magnum opus", the history of the family, compiled from old letters she found in the archives. I fear she did not receive all the encouragement she deserved in this work. I remember much resenting the fact that every evening was spent poring over scraps of paper covered with illegible writing, when I felt she should have been playing with us.'

Given the feeling of the Newtons for the place, it is odd that they swept away the early Georgian celebration of family history in the hall, with its echoes of the first Peter Legh's presence at Crecy, and replaced it with a blander, if more fashionable, Georgian Revival interior designed by Amadée Joubert, with rather bilious brown woodwork and a good deal of gilding to set off three outstanding Mortlake tapestries telling the story of *Hero and Leander*. The article, published on August 19, 1905, does not mention that the hall had been recently redone, nor does it give the date of the dining room, which was a clever Lewis Wyatt version of a late seventeenth century interior but with the walls subsequently painted light green by Joubert.

93 *Mortlake tapestries in the Edwardian front hall*

Treasurer's House

YORK

This is one of the houses that illustrates how Edward Hudson's ideas about *Country Life* related to the mood of the time. In 1896 Frank Green, a member of a West Riding family of inventive industrialists and for many years the driving force in the family firm, started to buy up the three portions of the house and entrusted its restoration to Temple Moore. It was illustrated in *Country Life* on February 17, 1906, when the author was at pains to say that it was not an SPAB job: 'The restoration is not put forward as faultless, but nothing was done without authority from evidences left. It is right to leave all old work untouched, if possible; but this cannot always be done. . . . The main object was to give an idea of the rooms and furniture of various periods, while it also

endeavoured to make the house inhabitable . . . it is a very notable work of artistic re-construction.'

The didactic approach to furnishing and decoration, with rooms of different periods being furnished in contemporary styles, must have been a fairly novel one at that time, and in 1922 Christopher Hussey pointed out that Frank Green was 'one of the pioneers of the present taste for beautiful furniture.'

When he gave the house to the National Trust in 1930, he laid down instructions about not altering the house or its arrangement. In *Ancestral Voices* James Lees-Milne records a visit to him in 1943, when he was berated by the old man: 'Was he to understand that someone had dared, had dared to shift the furniture in one of the rooms? Did I not realise that he had put little studs in the floors to mark the precise spot on which every single piece of furniture in the house was to stand?' I did. 'Then no piece was ever to be shifted therefore . . .'

94. (Above) *The hall from the east*

95. (Opposite above) *The view from the Georgian drawing room to the Restoration Chamber*

96. (Opposite below) *The Georgian staircase. The bold painted wallpaper supplied by Bodley and Garner no longer exists. The photograph is reproduced from a copy negative*

Welbeck Abbey

NOTTINGHAMSHIRE

The *Country Life* photographs, published on April 21, 1906, show the house after its restoration for the 6th Duke of Portland in 1900-1902. The Duke was the brother of Lady Ottoline Morell, who wrote of him: 'The aim of my eldest brother was his family should be a credit to him, but he never considered that there should be any intellectual or unconventional distinction. His carriages were to be the smartest in England, his shooting was to be the best shooting in England, his postillions were to be the best turned out.'

Welbeck as he had inherited it ten years earlier from his eccentric reclusive cousin had been in a strange state. The 5th Duke of Portland had devoted his resources to the construction of a series of sunk rooms and underground corridors, but he left the main house virtually unusable. Lady Ottoline describes how when they arrived at Welbeck on her brother's succession in 1879, 'the hall was without a floor and here also planks had been laid to allow us to enter. All the rooms were painted pink, and the large drawing rooms decorated in gold; but no furniture or pictures were to be seen . . . lovely pieces of rose-coloured Gobelins emerged from long tin cases. How well I remember the smell of peppercorns tumbling on the floor as these ornate rolls of tapestry were spread out before us.'

The tapestries had been ordered by the 3rd Duke of Portland in 1783.

Given that strange history and the earlier history of alterations and rebuildings, it is not surprising that the building never pulled together. Its most interesting eighteenth-century room to survive is the Gothic Hall, built by the Countess of Oxford in the late 1740s. To Mrs Delany, 'for workmanship in the true Gothick taste the Great hall exceeds everything I have seen of the kind.' But to the writer in 1906 it was just 'a curious example of the eighteenth century taste for toy shop Gothic, the fan tracery of the ceiling being stucco upon basket-work.' Given that view, it is not surprising that Sir Ernest George's alterations were unsympathetic.

97. Gobelin tapestry in the Red Drawing Room

98. *The Gothic Hall. The fan vault and the overmantel date from the late 1740s*

Nostell Priory
YORKSHIRE

It is extraordinary to find that when Nostell was first described in *Country Life* on April 27, 1907, Robert Adam was still so out of favour that the author of the article could write 'vast as the house's bulk may be, it was not large enough for the fancy of Sir Rowland's son, who had designs from Adam for four new wings, of which only one was finished when his death brought

reason to Nostell. This baronet bought many of the pictures which are the chief treasures of the house.' On the other hand in *English Homes* III (1909) it describes how Chippendale, perhaps because he was a Yorkshireman, was so admired that 'in the drawer of the library-table – itself one of his finest productions – is the great cabinet-maker's account for the furniture which he supplied in great abundance for Nostell.' By 1914, when the house was photographed again, the furniture had been rearranged and the late Victorian clutter cleared away; and the saloon (as can be seen from fig. 2), looked much as it does today.

99. *Late Victorian arrangement of the saloon. Its appearance in 1914 can be seen in Fig 2*

Houghton Hall

NORFOLK

'This quite remarkable specimen of a Georgian house, built, decorated and furnished at one time by one man, has never been adequately held as the chief seat of a wealthy and influential owner.' So wrote the author of the first article on Houghton published on July 27 and August 3, 1907, when it was not occupied by the Marquess of Cholmondeley but leased to Lieutenant Colonel Ralph Vivian. 'Bad times brought it into the market in 1883, but the offer of £300,000 for the house and its 10,000 acre estate was not accepted.'

In 1919, when the house became vacant, Lord Cholmondeley's heir, the Earl of Rocksavage, and his wife went to live there, and it remains Lady Cholmondely's home today. Thus Houghton has been more than 'adequately held' for almost seventy years. The photograph of the Saloon shows part of one of the large canvasses painted for the room by Cipriani after the 3rd Earl of Orford, sold Sir Robert's collection of pictures to Catherine the Great in 1779.

100. *The saloon door. Beside it hangs one of the Cipriani canvases painted for the room about 1780*

Iford Manor

THE GREAT PARLOUR

'I well remember, when on a bicycle tour, happening upon the place standing half derelict, and being charmed, even in the condition in which I found it, by its splendid hanging woods, its stately terrace walk, its interesting house with so much history in a medley of styles.' So wrote Avray Tipping on September 28, 1907, his description conjuring up the way country house enthusiasts, both architects and antiquarians, rediscovered England. By 1907 Iford was the home of a close friend, H.A. Peto (1854-1933), a partner of Sir Ernest George from 1881-1890. Iford provided a romantic setting for his architectural gardening, its formal bones lending themselves to the display of fragments of buildings and sculpture found in the course of his extensive travels. Within the house there was a simi-lar romantic, eclectic approach, as could be seen in the Great Parlour (reproduced here in a print from a copy negative): 'That his quick and simple conversion of a most uncompromisingly mid Victorian drawing room is a meet and proper setting for his fine Renascence furniture is obvious to those who glance at the illustration of the great parlour.'

Tipping wrote again on the house in August, 1922, when he illustrated the Hall, formed out of 'a dining room of such depressingly Victorian get-up that for some years Mr Peto made use of it merely as a store room.' Many years later Ralph Edwards described Peto as 'the British aesthete – in pose, appearance and voice. Verging on old age when I met him, he had been granted plenty of time to study the part. I recall him at dinner in Dorset Square [Tipping's house] with his fastidious air and mincing gait, cambric ruffles at his wrists, his manner and deportment evoking contemporary descriptions of Horace Walpole.'

101. (Opposite above) *The great parlour in 1907*

102. (Opposite below) *The garden hall in 1907*

103. (Below) *The h all in 1922*

Hursley Park

HAMPSHIRE

Hursley was one of the Edwardian country houses that owed its aggrandisement to an American fortune. In 1905 the medium-sized eighteenth-century house, probably designed by John James, was bought by Sir George Cooper and greatly enlarged. Born in Scotland in 1856, he married in 1887 Mary Smith from Illinois. In 1902 they took 26 Grosvenor Square and had the interior done up in the height of fashion by Howard & Sons (Bedford Lemere's photographs are included in *The Opulent Eye*). For Hursley they turned to A. Marshall Mackenzie, the architect of the Waldorf Hotel, who was a kinsman. He designed the additions to follow the style of the original house, as can be seen when the first article by Horace Annesley Vachell on December 13, 1902, is compared with the second one on October 23, 1907. The interior, however, was decorated in a variety of styles, a Wren hall, a Georgian drawing room, a Jacobean boudoir, a

French ballroom with tapestries; and Duveen advised on the purchase of eighteenth-century English portraits and works of art. The hall was fitted out with panelling from the chapel at Winchester College. *The Architectural Review* in 1905 recorded it cost 30,000 gns: 'We are afraid this deals too much with the commercial side to be of interest to you and your readers, but it undoubtedly shows the craving for anything in the way of antique work; and, of course, the fact of this being attributed to Grinling Gibbons has given it this fancy value.' It is revealing to discover quite how expensive such architectural interiors were at that time, and they invariably involved more alteration than was admitted to make them fit. In 1952 Sir George Cooper gave the panelling back to Winchester.

104. (Below) *Panelling from the chapel at Winchester College, in the hall*

105. (Opposite) *Beauvais tapestry in the Louis XV ballroom*

Boughton House
NORTHAMPTONSHIRE

Boughton remains one of the most magical of all English country houses, and that is so partly due to the way that it has been awakened from its sleep in this century. In 1909 Boughton struck the author of the article on January 30 as 'a place in decay', and 'yet [it] is open to question whether this decay is not more agreeable and sympathetic than might have been its maintainance as a great ducal residence, with the succession of alterations and additions . . . It might be the home of one who has slept longer even than Rip Van Winkle . . . ' In fact in

106. (Opposite) *The great hall before its restoration in 1910*

107. (Below) *Mortlake tapestry in the Second State Room*

the 1890s the 6th Duke of Buccleuch had considered a major 'restoration' by Arthur Blomfield of the Great Hall, which would have entailed the removal of the 1st Duke of Montagu's painted ceiling and its refitting in the Tudor style. Why the Hall should have decayed is puzzling, because the rest of the great house was kept up. The 1909 photographs are of interest because they show the giant order of pilasters on the window wall, a detail reminiscent of the Great Hall at Drayton, a few miles away, which was refitted by William Talman. Shortly after the *Country Life* article appeared, the repair of the Hall was taken in hand, and the present effective arrangement of panelling and tapestries was introduced, but the pilasters were removed. At that time the state rooms still contained the bed that is now in the Victoria and Albert Museum, but it is indicative of how long it is since they have been used as they were intended, that they are only numbered, their original names having been generally forgotten.

Blenheim Palace
OXFORDSHIRE

Although the state rooms at Boughton and Blenheim are only a generation apart in date, Blenheim in 1909 was the opposite of Boughton, with it splendours recently enriched in an international Louis style. The article of June 5, 1909 however, makes no mention of the altera-

tions carried out for the 9th Duke of Marlborough and his American wife, Consuelo Vanderbilt. The Duke saw his redecoration as part of the restoration of Blenheim after the depredations of the previous two generations. As a result of the Blenheim Settled Estates Act in 1881-82 the 7th Duke had sold the Sunderland Library, and the 8th Duke had sold not only the great collection of pictures but also furniture and china. Thus the 9th Duke, who succeeded in 1892, felt the need to marry money, while Mrs W.K. Vanderbilt was determined that

108. *The long gallery*

109. (Opposite)
The Second State Room with one of the great Duke of Marlborough's Battle tapestries

he should marry her daughter, Consuelo. The marriage, which took place in 1895, was not a happy one, as Consuelo Balsan, (as the Duchess eventually became), described in *The Glitter and The Gold* (1953). However, with her fortune the Duke was able to give the famous Marlborough battle tapestries a setting that echoed Versailles, stylistically a logical idea but surely one that would have been abhorrent to Duchess Sarah. Oddly he did not record who carried out the architectural embellishments and supplied copies of Louis XIV chandeliers, torcheres and armchairs, but later in 1925, in a letter to Duchene, who restored the parterres, wrote 'When I was young and uninformed I put French decoration into

the three state rooms here. The rooms have English proportions . . . and the result is that the French decoration is quite out of scale . . . and leaves a very unpleasant impression on those with trained eyes.' If they give what strikes as a rather International American gloss to the rooms, the Duke almost inevitably went to Sargent in 1905 for a group portrait to balance the Reynolds of the Duke and his family that is much the grandest picture of its time. Instead, however, of reflecting recent changes in the house in the background, Sargent suggested the classicism of Wren and Vanbrugh, the effect being curiously like Lutyens.

Holme Lacy

HEREFORDSHIRE

It was probably not coincidence that the article on the house published on June 12 and 19, 1909, appeared at the same time as the whole place was put on the market by the 10th Earl of Chesterfield; and, as has happened on a number of occasions since, the articles were prompted by a desire to make a record before it was too late. Holme Lacy was noted for the richness of its Charles II plasterwork and its Gibbons carvings, and the author (probably Tipping) realised that it was almost certain that the latter would be removed. Lord Chesterfield, who had inherited in 1887, married in 1900 a daughter of the 1st Lord Nunburnholme, and they did a certain amount to the house, including joining two rooms with particularly fine ceilings and carved overmantels to form a long drawing room, an idea that they were to repeat

in 1917 at Beningbrough, which was where they moved to (figs. 205, 206). They also had the State Bed restored. According to the article of June 19, 1909, 'it had for long been taken to pieces and stored away. The portions were sent to Messrs Morant, who had the crimson damask with which it was covered reproduced, and the curtains and lower part are composed of the reproduction, the tester still almost entirely retaining the original covering. The work was done with all the care and fidelity for which Messrs Morant are celebrated . . . . ' Morants were an old-established firm who worked in a number of country houses at the beginning of the century, carrying out careful restorations, on occasion – as at Dunham Massey – with the advice of Percy Macquoid.

In 1915 Morants merged with Lenygon, the antique dealers with showrooms in a fine house in Old Burlington Street. The combined firm did a great deal of excellent period decoration and restoration that had a marked influence on taste after the First World War.

111. (Below) *The overmantel at the west end of the drawing room*

112. (Opposite) *The overmantel at the east end of the drawing room*

110. *The state bed*

139

Erddig

NORTH WALES

The saving of this house by the National Trust in the 1970s involved many stories of eccentricity, and, indeed, part of the reason for the effort put into the lengthy negotiations and afterwards into the processes of restoration were the strange personalities of the last two Yorkes of Erddig, Simon and his younger brother Philip, who inherited in 1966 and was the eventual donor of the property. Merlin Waterson's *The Servants' Hall* (1980) gives a vivid, insider's view of the house at that time and the deep impression that Erddig and Philip Yorke made on him.

The way a house so rich in fascinating objects could plunge downhill so quickly was very poignant and disturbing; and it was ironical that much of the trouble was caused by the pillar of coal on which it had stood being cut away after nationalisation, so causing subsidence that virtually broke its back. It became a forgotten house except to enthusiasts, who have many stories of visits to Philip Yorke, of his reminiscing about his days as an actor in rep over tea and highly coloured cake in the old servants' hall, of Georgian salvers being used as reflectors for gas lights, and sheep, employed instead of gardeners to 'mow' the lawns, getting into the drawing room and butting their own images in the looking glass door.

Yet in 1909, when the house was illustrated for the first time on November 27, its importance was fully recognised, and its documents had been carefully gone through. A few years later they were used by Albinia Lucy Cust in her two volumes of *Chronicles of Erthig on the Dyke* (1914). It was realised that they 'help to place Erddig in the front rank of houses stored with examples of the decorative arts that have the combined merit of aesthetic value and family association.' When it came to restoration some sixty years later, those photographs (those of the saloon and the tapestry room are taken from copy negatives), and a second set taken for articles by Margaret Jourdain published in 1930, were among the visual evidence that enabled the house to be arranged more or less as it was when Simon Yorke inherited it in 1922.

113. (Below) *The servants hall.*

114. (Opposite above) *The panelled saloon*

115. (Opposite below) *The Tapestry Room. The tapestry was delivered in 1721*

116. (Above) *The east side of the hall at Adcote*

117. (Opposite) *The Oak Parlour at Mathern Palace*

Adcote

SHROPSHIRE

Looking at the photographs of the exterior and interior of this house (the view of the hall is taken from a copy negative) and reading the article published on December 25, 1909, one wonders to what extent Edward Hudson discussed his plans not only with Tipping and Weaver, but with Lutyens, who from 1910 had his office in the next door house in Queen Anne's Gate. Are there echoes of their conversations in the remarks that Norman Shaw is 'now gladly acknowledged as a master by many of the more thoughtful architects of to-day.' and that Adcote was 'not merely a house. It is a very important chapter in the book of the evolution of our recent domestic architecture'? The whole article, in fact, is most revealing about the attitudes of the time it was written: 'The idea of Adcote was that it should link with the England of the past, belong to the geology and geography of Shropshire and yet be the outcome of the ethics of to-day.'

Mathern Palace

MONMOUTHSHIRE

This was the first house of H. Avray Tipping to be illustrated in *Country Life*, on November 19, 1910. The place owed its grand name to its ownership by the mediaeval Bishops of Llandaff, but by the eighteenth century it had declined into being a farm house. Since it 'was by no means convenient and comfortable habitation even for farmers,' they had moved out and put labourers into it; and 'It was only the agricultural depression of twenty years ago that brought him back to its leaking roofs and wind-swept rooms.' Thus much of the building had disappeared or was in ruins when Tipping discovered it and decided in 1894 to make it habitable. When it was photographed in 1910 the emphasis of the illustrations is on the exterior and the garden, which was Tipping's great enthusiasm, but they include one view of the Oak Parlour.

Chequers Court

BUCKINGHAMSHIRE

The story of how Chequers became the country house of British Prime Ministers is a strange and in some ways sad one. Arthur Lee had an unhappy, deprived childhood, being brought up by a well-to-do but unfeeling spinster and having little contact with his real family. It was partly to escape from her that he went to Canada as an ambitious and adventure-seeking young Artillery officer. In America he met his future wife, Ruth Moore, whom he eventually married in 1899. With the aid of her fortune he was able to return to England and become a Member of Parliament. In 1909 they took a lease of Chequers, discovered through the advertisement pages of *Country Life*, completing its restoration with the aid of Reginald Blomfield. Five years later, when the owner was killed, they decided to secure the freehold and also they managed to acquire from a pawnbroker the Cromwell relics that belonged to the house. That led them to think of its future and to the idea of bequeathing it as a residence for future Prime Ministers, a plan formalised in the Chequers Estate Act of 1917. In 1921 they made the generous decision to hand over the house and endowment straight away; and they started a new life. And in the process they established a precedent for the National Trust's Country Houses Scheme.

Although in the eyes of the world Arthur Lee's career was a story of success inspired by noble and patriotic ideas, and recognised publicly by his being created Viscount Lee of Fareham, his own account in *A Good Innings*, published in 1974 with an introduction by Alan Clark, reveals an ultimately disappointed man.

For much of the second part of his life, when he was out of the centre of public life, he devoted a great deal of time to collecting pictures and also to the establishment of the teaching of art history in England. In 1929 he explained his scheme to Samuel Courtauld,

118. *The Edwardian great hall in the courtyard*

119. (Opposite) *The library*

who generously agreed to back it, and four years later he finally achieved his target figure for endowment for the Institute that bears Courtauld's name and to which he bequeathed his own collection. So the nation owes him and his wife a double debt.

The discovery of Chequers was the fulfilment of a romantic pipe-dream as well as a demonstration of Lee's success, and its restoration was typical of its period: Victorian trimmings were stripped away, rooms were repanelled and a now Edwardian-seeming Great Hall, comparable with that of Hill Hall, drawing on the various periods in the house for its detailing, was formed in a courtyard. The appearance of the gallery in recent years can be seen in *The Inspiration of the Past*, plate LXIV.

Tipping, who wrote the first article on December 31, 1910, also designed the garden and the architectural setting of the house, and in the third of a second series of articles on October 20, 1917, he quoted a letter from Lady Lee, 'We are delighted on every ground but one that you are writing the new articles on Chequers, but we should feel it is misfortune if the merits of the gardens round the house should be slurred over merely because you designed them. At the same time, we understand your reluctance to write about your own work, and only wish that the task could have been entrusted to other hands.' Her letter incidentally is dated October 7, the date of the first of the series of articles, and it shows how even then articles went straight from pot to consumer.

Ardenrun Place

SURREY

In 1910 *Country Life* began to include recent houses in its main series on Country Homes, almost certainly as a result of the arrival of Lawrence Weaver on the staff. Ardenrun, built in 1906-1909, was designed by Ernest Newton, whose houses were perhaps the most understated of the late nineteenth and early twentieth century. As the article on January 21, 1911, said: 'he has been inspired by the work of the last half of the seventeenth century. It is doubtful whether there is

120. (Opposite) *The hall and Caroline-style staircase balustrade*

121. (Below) *French decoration in the Tapestry Hall*

any period of our national architecture which produced buildings so satisfying as the country houses of that time.' Indeed a drawing of it in perspective by F.L. Griggs strongly recalls Groombridge Place, and Alick G. Horswell's watercolour also has a romantic softness about it (both reproduced in Clive Aslet's *The Last Country Houses*), whereas in photographs the house is less appealing, appearing rather hard. A fusion of the late seventeenth and early eighteenth century styles inspired Newton's treatment of the hall and staircase and also the dining room, but in a typically Edwardian way there was a desire for variety and a dash of French so the decoration of the Tapestry Hall and the Drawing Room were 'entrusted to a Parisian firm to be carried out in a French manner, and it necessarily looks a little thin after the robust English treatment of the staircase hall.' The house was burned in 1933.

Quenby Hall

LEICESTERSHIRE

In recent years many of the early twentieth-century restorations recorded in *Country Life* have started to develop their own particular romantic fascination. Among them is Quenby, which in 1911 belonged to Mrs Edward Greaves, the sister of Morgan Stuart Williams, who in 1901 began the restoration of St Donat's Castle with the aid of Garner and continued after 1906 with Bodley. Mrs Greaves started off with Bodley and then continued with J.A. Gotch from Kettering. As might be expected from those two architects the work was carefully done, but it was not at all an easy task because of earlier alterations. Her most ambitious operation was to recreate the Great Parlour on the first floor. That involved putting back the floor taken out in the eighteenth century, bringing the chimneypiece from the Hall below and panelling out of the attics while copying the ceiling of the ball room at Knole. The author of the articles on October 14 and 21 wrote 'Recently, a twentieth century "restorer" has taken the place in hand; but a restorer of the best and most informed kind; who has done visibly little, though materially much' . . . and he went on to praise her 'skill and taste in either collecting old fittings and furniture or having them reproduced adequately, and in bringing them together as a thoroughly handsome whole.' Like so many of her generation Mrs Greaves had a feeling for textures and stuffs, and while it is no surprise to find her using tapestry it is surely more surprising to see rush matting in the hall.

123. (Opposite above) *A bedroom in the William III manner*

122. (Below) *The restored great parlour*

124. (Opposite below) *The Georgian kitchen*

Knole
KENT

Today Edwardian Knole lives on in V. Sackville-West's evocative novel *The Edwardians* with its marvellous descriptions of the house and its life. So it may come as a surprise to read of the understanding of the house shown by her parents that was acknowledged by Tipping in his articles in 1912: 'They bring to the preservation of its true character an informed knowledge and a warm affection.' That is confirmed by Sir Horace Rumbold in *Final Recollections of a Diplomatist* (1905), who wrote: 'To those laudable instincts of its former inmates must now be added the happy circumstance that the splendid place and the treasures that fill it are committed to the care of Mrs Sackville-West, whose exceptional understanding of pictures, ancient furniture, and antique *bric a brac* of all kinds, united to perfect taste, is such as to make her the most competent of custodians for the stately possession that first came to the family in Elizabethan days . . . .' Susan Mary Alsop in her life of the late Lady Sackville published in 1978 quotes from her *Book of Reminiscences* (1922): 'I got from Mama my love of beautiful things and of great comfort. I had a fine field to work upon at Knole. The first things I did, after re-arranging the furniture and putting in the Garretts or Barracks the early Victorian horrors, was to begin to make Bath-Rooms. . . . . I enjoyed immensely installing the electric light at Knole and putting in all the modern improvements I could. . . . Everybody says that I made Knole the most comfortable large house in England, uniting the beauties of Windsor Castle with the comforts of the Ritz and I never spoilt the old character of Knole.' It seems to have been her idea to increase the opening of the house to three afternoons a week and to advertise it, and her husband's 1906 edition of the guidebook records the stripping of the panelling in the Great Hall in 1904 and the lighting of the pictures. Among the illustrations in the 1912 articles is one of Lady Sackville's Sitting Room (shown here in a print from a copy negative) on the first floor of the Bourchier gatehouse which has a certain curiosity, because Lady Sackville was one of the first ladies to have a decorating shop in London.

125. (Below)) *The screen in the great hall*
126. (Opposite above) *The Kings Room with its bed of gold and silver brocade*
127. (Opposite below) *Lady Sackville's sitting room. Her eagle eye recognised the mother of pearl and polychrome boulle bureau sold at Christies in 1987 for almost £1,250,000*

Little Ridge

WILTSHIRE

While Lutyens has never dropped completely out of favour, at least at *Country Life*, it is only very recently that his contemporary Detmar Blow (1857-1939) has started to receive attention again, and his houses in the Avon and Wylye valleys have been compared with those of Lutyens in West Surrey. Meeting Ruskin by chance in Abbeville in 1888, Blow was introduced by him to Burne Jones, Morris and probably Webb, and he joined the SPAB in 1890, the year before Gimson. As a result of that he worked under Philip Webb on the repair of East Knoyle church in 1892-93 and came to know the circle of the Wyndhams at Clouds. Little Ridge, or Fonthill House as it was called later, was designed for Hugh Morrison in 1904 and extended in 1906. It was built out of the remains of a sixteenth-century manor house that stood about three miles away on another part of the Fonthill estate, and was moved stone by stone. It was so sensitively done, with the aid of local masons, carpenters and plasterers still working in the traditional manner, that the author of the *Country Life* article on October 12, 1912 could write: 'Thus could Mr Blow feel secure that the fragmentary skeleton of the Berwick St Leonard manor house would be revivified and re-clothed as a modern house on a modern site and yet not lose its ancient savour.' And as Gervase Jackson-Stops wrote on July 3, 1986: 'The rooms at Little Ridge perfectly expressed his taste, more subtle than Lutyens and less folksy than many of the Broadway school.' Of the library the author wrote 'The recessed bookcases, the pilasters framing the marble mantel-piece, the cornice and beams with their dentil enrichment, give that reposeful dignity so right in a library.' Sadly the house was demolished in 1972, too soon to have received the reassessment that might have reprieved it.

128. (Below) *The library at Little Ridge*

129. (Opposite) *The Louis revival drawing room at Cliveden. Later the room became English Georgian*

Cliveden
BUCKINGHAMSHIRE

When Cliveden ceased to be lived in by the Astor family, it quickly began to feel like a hotel, and it seems appropriate that it should have become one, in particular one intended to appeal to Americans, because it was probably the first great English house to be bought by an American. The Barry *palazzo* on its superb seventeenth-century site was bought from the Duke of Westminster in 1893 by William Waldorf Astor, who had decided to settle in England four years earlier. With the aid of Pearson he remodelled the interior in a 5th Avenue/Long Island eclectic style that combined echoes of Antiquity, the Italian Renaissance, French Gothic, the Ancien Regime and the Adams Revival; and by an odd coincidence he bought back for the house tapestries that had been there in the eighteenth century. When his son Waldorf married in 1906, he gave him the house as a wedding present. Many years later, in 1951, his daughter-in-law, Nancy, Lady Astor, recalled: 'The keynote of the place when I took over was splendid gloom. Tapestries and ancient leather furniture filled most of the rooms. The place looked better when I had put in books and chintz curtains and covers, and flowers.' She had the Italian mosaic floor removed from the hall and the painted ceiling in the dining room covered, but fortunately she did not touch the beautiful Rococo boiserie from Chateau d'Asnières in the dining room installed in 1897. Her most important change was to water down the Drawing Room, removing the columns and the decorated ceiling and leaving only the pilasters and entablature. The date of this is not known, but possibly Lutyens had a hand in it, because the chimneypieces could well be his. Further reversible modifications were carried out in 1985, when it became the dining room of the hotel. Here the room is shown as it appeared in *Country Life* on December 14, 1912. There is a vivid account of Cliveden between the wars in *Tribal Feeling* by Michael Astor, one of the sons of the 2nd Lord Astor.

Normanton

RUTLAND

Normanton is one of the lost houses of the twentieth century, its site now covered by Rutland Water, with the classical church surviving on a headland pointing into the lake as in a capriccio by Canaletto. So it is fortunate that the house was photographed for an article published in *Country Life* on February 8, 1913 about seven years before it was demolished. The house had been built about 1735-40 by Sir John Heathcote to the designs of Henry Joynes, and was subsequently altered on several occasions. The family fortune had been founded by the first Sir Gilbert Heathcote, one of the founders of the Bank of England and Lord Mayor of London in 1711. It is thought that he ordered the state bed, which is now at Buscot Park, and also the tapestries from Joshua Morris in Soho in the 1720s that were hung in the new state bedroom at Normanton and are now at Grimsthorpe. In the late eighteenth century the back drawing room was redecorated, the scheme including 'laughing and sporting cupids in chiaroscuro' painted in grey on crimson silk, which, the author of the 1913 article remarked, were the family racing colours.

130. *Soho tapestries in the State Bedroom*

131. (Opposite above) *Chinese wallpaper in a bedroom*

132. (Opposite below) *The Back Drawing Room*

Lindisfarne Castle

NORTHUMBERLAND

Edward Hudson discovered the unoccupied castle on a visit to Lindisfarne with P. Anderson Graham, the Editor of *Country Life* and the author of *Highways and Byeways in Northumbria*. Fired with enthusiasm, Hudson set about acquiring it from the Crown and in 1902 he summoned Lutyens to adapt it for him. Lutyens' approach to the job was free, and it may have been partly for that reason that the article in *Country Life* on June 7, 1913, was written by Anderson Graham rather than by Tipping. He did not sign it but revealed that he was 'the scribe who indites these annals'. Quite rightly he praised Hudson's gift for arrangement: 'Exactly the right number of rightly selected pieces of furniture, mostly of the English or Flemish early seventeenth century oaken type, are there to complete the picture.' The approach was strongly pictorial and it is interesting to see that borne out in a series of photographs of Barbara Lutyens (fig. 20) taken when the family were on holiday there in 1906, which are artistic compositions in the manner of seventeenth century Dutch paintings, with echoes of Vermeer and de Hooch. Lindisfarne proved inconveniently far from London, and as early as 1904 or 1905 Hudson considered buying Lympne Castle on the coast of Kent, but was then pipped to the post. After his godson, Billy Congreve, to whom he intended to leave the castle, was killed in the first world war, he lost interest in it, and in 1921 he sold it. It was given to the National Trust in 1944 by Sir Edward Stein, who had bought it with some of Hudson's furniture, so it still has some of the character that it had before the First War.

133. (Opposite above) *The gallery stairway*

134. (Opposite below) *The gallery looking east*

135. (Below) *The Ship Room. Lutyens inserted the big hearth and new windows in an existing vaulted chamber*

Kedleston Hall
DERBYSHIRE

The articles published on December 20 and 27, 1913, show the house at the end of the lifetime of the 4th Lord Scarsdale, the father of Marquess Curzon, and it is perhaps a pity that they were not written a few years later, so describing Lord Curzon's restoration with A.S.G. Butler. The articles are signed J., which, combined with the special attention given to the furniture, suggests Margaret Jourdain. Whoever it was, was aware of the Adam drawings and the documentation of the picture collection formed by the builder mainly in the 1750s. 'One remarkable feature of the collection of Old Masters made for Kedleston is that it remains intact, not a single picture having been parted with during the ensuing 150 years.' That gives a particular value to the arrangement in the drawing room as recorded in the photograph, because it shows how large pictures were set off with smaller ones, an arrangement that had all but disappeared by the time Kedleston was next described in *Country Life* in 1978. The 1913 photograph also shows the walls as having lost their damask hangings: the present ones are a copy of what Lord Curzon replaced, following the Chinese peony pattern on the merman sofas and recorded in other contemporary houses. That was typical of Lord Curzon's passionate concern for detail and research, but then Kedleston and all it stood for in historic as well as aesthetic terms was a great source of inspiration to him. As he wrote to the Archbishop of York, 'I will not disguise from you, my dear Lang, what pleasure it gives me, as the years advance, to see my friends inhabiting spacious places.'

136. (Below) *The drawing room. The walls were later rehung with damask by Lord Curzon*

137. (Opposite above) *The dining room*

138. (Opposite below) *The kitchen in the north-west wing*

159

Brinsop Court

HEREFORDSHIRE

Tipping not only worked on his own houses and gardens, but from time to time advised friends and acquaintances. Presumably that was why he was asked by Mr Hubert Astley and Lady Sutton (who, when she remarried, retained the name and style of her first marriage), who bought Brinsop, a mediaeval moated house laid out round a court yard and then in a state of advanced decay, to take charge of its remodelling. They intended it to be a combination of repairs that would satisfy the SPAB, who were consulted and gave their approval, and new building. In the article published on November 7, 1914, Martin Conway wrote: 'We must preserve all its old features intact that can by any ingenuity be retained, but having done that, we are free to add

what we please, provided that the result is beautiful.' (That was what he himself had been doing at Allington Castle.) Certainly Tipping's work was well researched, but photographs suggest that it did not really come alive. The Solar, for instance, was made into the library, with panelling and an overmantel brought in from Mildmay House, Clerkenwell, and its ceiling copied from one at Chastleton. The Oak Parlour (shown here in a photograph taken from a copy negative) was a new room: 'The old lamp room and other closets that used to adjoin the kitchen on the South were taken away and the space thus unencumbered became a kind of lobby, separated from the larger room by a balustraded screen with a wide opening in the midst.' That screen was surely inspired by one made by Lorimer for Earlshall (fig. 88).

139. (Below) *The Oak Parlour. Tipping copied the screen from Earlshall (Fig 88)*

140. (Opposite) *The fourteenth-century banquetting hall*

Mounton House

MONMOUTHSHIRE

This was Tipping's second country house, and, according to Martin Conway, who wrote about it in *Country Life* on February 13, 1915, he had started the garden several years before he began building, because he had 'a craving for a larger field of activity' than was offered by Mathern, which was only a mile or so away. Construction began in 1911 and Tipping moved into the house in 1912. Martin Conway pointed out that 'few architects have had the chance to build so large a house for themselves,' but he did not mention the name of Tipping's professional collaborator, E.C. Francis. As he said, 'At no time in England has so much attention been devoted to the maintenance and repair of old houses as during the last quarter of the century. The study of the history of domestic architecture has been almost a passion with some. At the same time, there has flourished an equal delight in house-building and garden making.

The telephone and the motor car have revolutionised country life; electrical and other appliances have invaded the house. All sorts of new conveniences and labour saving contrivances have been placed at our disposal, while simultaneously there has been a shrinkage of domestic labour and a steady rise in the demand for its comfortable and even luxurious accommodation.' If the style of the exterior of Mounton was loosely vernacular, the interior was in a variety of styles. Again there was an Oak Parlour furnished with English and continental furniture, and Martin Conway was particularly taken with its electric light fittings, 'each globe being partially smothered in a tassel of coloured and knotted silks, like the Jacobean tassles to be seen, for instance, on furniture at Knole. . . . The dining room is planned and decorated in the style of the late eighteenth century because many of its chief features – doors, marble chimneypieces, sideboards and chairs – were heirlooms or, at any rate, possessions of the owner.' In contrast to that room, Tipping's bedroom was Old English with plasterwork copied from the ceiling in the gallery at Chastleton.

141. *H. Avray Tipping's bedroom. He copied the plaster work from Chastleton as he had at Brinsop Court*

142. (Opposite below) *The Oak Parlour. A development of his earlier room seen in Fig 117*

143. (Opposite above) *The dining room. The chimneypiece came from Brasted Court, his parents' Adam house in Kent, which he sold shortly before building Mounton.*

Raby Castle

DURHAM

Country Life has been illustrating houses for such a long time that many places have been described on more than one occasion, so that while the illustrations record visual alterations, the texts reflect the development of knowledge and changes in taste. It is, for instance, interesting to compare the two treatments of Raby Castle, the first by Tipping on December 4, 1915, and the second, fifty-four years later, by Alistair Rowan in 1969. In both attention was directed at the kitchen which was part of the work of the 3rd Lord Neville, a great soldier of the time of Edward III, who was granted licence to crenellate in 1378 and was the man principally responsible for the mediaeval form of Raby. The kitchen is now attributed to John Lewyn, the principal mason in charge of Durham Cathedral, and, as Alistair Rowan wrote, 'It is one of the most memorable mediaeval rooms in Britain, and it is also one of the most perfect.'

144. *The fourteenth-century kitchen*

Buscot Park

BERKSHIRE

In 1889 Buscot was bought by Alexander Henderson, later 1st Lord Faringdon (1850-1934), a railway magnate active here and in South America and one of the great business entrepreneurs of his age. He entered the House of Commons in 1898, was made a baronet in 1902 and created a baron in 1916. He formed a large collection of nineteenth-century pictures, which were mostly sold after his death, and he also acquired fine Old Masters, which remain at Buscot. The Briar Rose series of paintings were part of that first collection. Burne Jones had begun to paint the story as early at 1871, but it was only in 1890 that he exhibited the final four paintings at Agnews, which were brought by Alexander Henderson before they went on show. When the artist was staying with Morris at Kelmscott he visited the house and, not being satisfied with their setting, he designed a framework of giltwood with some extra painted slips to give unity to the pictures. Lord Faringdon also laid out an elaborate garden designed by Harold Peto, which was the main theme of the article published on October 21st, 1916.

145. *The Briar Rose Room*

Hill Hall

Essex

After a visit to Hill Hall in 1912, Henry James wrote, 'I have made ... this much dash into the world. It is the world of the wonderful and delightful Mrs Charles Hunter, whom you may know (long my very kind friends) and all swimming just now in a sea of music. John Sargent (as much a player as a painter), Percy Grainger, Roger Quilter, Wilfred de Glehn and others.' Lutyens who went there two years earlier wrote. 'Sargents galore, Mancinis and other modern artists. Italian furniture and silks. Alas, Blomfield is the architect.'

Mrs Hunter, the wife of a wealthy coal owner and the sister of Dame Ethel Smyth, the composer, only leased the house, which was half an hour from London, but with characteristic extravagance she did a great deal to it. Among the changes made by Blomfield in 1909 was the enrichment of the Great Hall, exchanging a simple arcade for columns, which were apparently marbled by Sargent, who was an old friend of Mrs Hunter. At the far end of it can be seen Sargent's portrait of her three daughters, which is not identified by Tipping in his articles in the spring of 1917. Clearly he did not feel at ease in the house, as can be gathered from such passages as: 'Venice, however, became the happy hunting ground of Mrs Charles Hunter in her search for furniture and fittings. English furniture of the age of Anne might have been preferable in an English house with so many characteristics of that age.' Of an 1851 wallpaper in a bedroom, he wrote 'The designing may be theatrical, the drawing defective and the colouring crude, but it possesses some distinction.' Clearly he did not share Henry James's enthusiasm.

146. (Below) *The dining room*

147. (Opposite) *Sargeant's portrait of Mrs Hunter's daughters in the hall*

Herstmonceaux Castle

SUSSEX

Surely one of the surprising strands in the history of the country house in the early twentieth century is the restoration of castles and their transformations into houses. Indeed, on July 21st, 1906, there was an advertisement in *Country Life* offering Herstmonceaux and 180 acres with the suggestion that 'a modern house might be erected without in any way marring the amenities of the castle'. Martin Conway, the restorer and recreator of Allington Castle, wrote about Colonel Claude Lowther's work here on March 2, 9 and 16, 1918. Colonel Lowther had a varied career, in the diplomatic service, as a Member of Parliament from 1900 to 1906 and from 1910 to 1918 and a soldier. Recommended for the VC in the South African War, he raised Lowther's Lambs in Sussex at the outbreak of the 1914 war and then three more battalions in 1915. Two years before the war he bought the ruins

of the castle, and began repairs, but the work was held up by the war and was then resumed afterwards. Of the interior Conway wrote: 'Colonel Lowther possesses an almost unique power of creating in every room he decorates an atmosphere of romance.'

Martin Conway wrote rather differently about his approach in *Episodes in a Varied Life* in 1932, explaining that the Colonel was inspired by what they were doing at Allington, deciding 'to undertake another castle rather than attack a monastic building. . . . he was more thorough than we were in the application of our principles. Frankly he cared nothing about archaeology or historical correctness. His lovely ruins were to be shaped by addition or removals into the most beautiful whole that he could devise.'

In May, 1929, the year of Lowther's death, Tipping revisited Herstmonceaux, and the views of the State Bedroom and the Ladies Bower come from that article. The great work of reconstruction however, was brought to a conclusion by Sir Paul Latham (illustrated in *Country Life* in November and December, 1935).

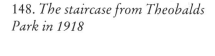

148. *The staircase from Theobalds Park in 1918*

149. (Opposite above) *The great bedroom in 1929. Tipping evidently did not trust himself to comment on the decoration in the article*

150. (Opposite below) *'The Ladies Bower' in 1929. Sir Paul Latham soon did away with the elaborate decoration and made a simpler drawing room*

Sledmere

YORKSHIRE

Sledmere as it appeared in 1897 was a cluttered Victorian house conceived by a progressive and informed Georgian. As rebuilt after the fire of 1911 it became a more spectacular and a much more complicated Edwardian country house. However, the article published on October 5, 1918, says little about Walter Brierley's restoration and extension of the house begun for Sir Tatton Sykes, who died in 1913, and completed for Sir Mark.

Sir Mark, born in 1879, was a fascinating figure: as a young man he travelled in Syria, Mesopotamia and Southern Kurdistan and from 1905 to 1907 served as an honorary attaché at the British Embassy in Constantinople. It was that early experience that explains his work in the First World War, when through the so-called Sykes-Picot pact of 1916 he played a major role in the defining of English, French and Russian interests in the Middle East. After that he served the Foreign Office as adviser on Near Eastern policy. He died in 1919.

The principal rooms were restored as carefully as possible, and since the pictures and furniture had been rescued, a convincing late eighteenth-century effect was re-created. However some changes were made: the original South Hall and staircase hall were thrown together to provide a huge central space in the manner of a grand hotel, while keeping to the original vocabulary of neo-classical ornament. A new Stone Hall-cum-smoking room was formed 'to give the impression of a guardroom by its bold and simple decoration,' which, while suggesting the possible influence of Lutyens on Brierley, relates rather oddly to the rest of the house. Also a remarkable Turkish Room, entirely decorated in tiles, was installed as a reflection of Sir Mark's own enthusiasm for that part of the the world. Here one of the simpler rooms is illustrated, the Bloodstock Room, because it is so expressive of the passion for horses that has run through most generations of the Sykes family, who continue to run the oldest stud in England, founded in 1801.

151. *Sporting pictures in the Bloodstock Room*

152. *Brierley's staircase hall*

Sutton Scarsdale

DERBYSHIRE

Today a motor-way provides a dramatic succession of views of Elizabethan Hardwick, Jacobean Bolsover and the ruins of early Georgian Sutton Scarsdale, and while readers of D.H. Lawrence probably associate the last of these with the story of *Lady Chatterley's Lover*, and Americans know it through rooms in the Philadelphia Museum, others have been introduced to it by Sacheverell Sitwell in *British Architects and Craftsmen*.

Margaret Jourdain wrote about the house in *Country Life* in 1919, when it was still the home of the Arkwrights, but, alas, the only complete room to be photographed was the entrance hall. The following year, when the place was put on the market, no buyer could be found, and so the house was sold off. Vandals got in, and the lead was taken off the roof. Then Sacheverell Sitwell takes up the story: 'While spending the autumn at my old home, in 1920, or soon after, word was brought

to us that there had been a sale at Sutton Scarsdale, and that my brother and myself had better go there . . . ' But it was too late. 'No purchaser would even buy the stone, and later, it was proposed to blow it up with gunpowder. . . When we saw it, the ceiling of the lower room had fallen in, so that there was the extraordinary spectacle of four Venetian mantlepieces, all of the richest work imaginable, richer, far, than anything in a Venetian palace, hanging in the air, with the remains of the coloured stucco in panels and niches upon the walls, and some fragments of the figures on the higher stucco ceiling.' The Sitwells wanted to save an upper chimney piece: 'But some days went by before a farm cart could be sent over to fetch it, and during that interval it had collapsed entirely and lay in little pieces on the floor.'

In the end, in 1955, when a final clearance of the site was threatened, Sir Osbert Sitwell bought the site in order to give the ruins a chance, and after his death they were taken into guardianship as an Ancient Monument.

153. *The entrance hall at Sutton Scarsdale*

Hamilton Palace

Avray Tipping's articles in 1919 were almost an obituary on this vast house of the Dukes of Hamilton and Brandon, which had been little used after the sales of 1882 and was no longer needed after a naval hospital moved out at the end of the First World War. 'The exaggerated grandeur of the great magnate of a century ago makes no appeal,' wrote Tipping, 'yet as a matter of sentiment, it is not only those immediately concerned to whom the passing away of a "stately house", with all its material splendour and manifold traditions, is a matter of real regret.' But it is striking that even he could not envisage the organised preservation of such a building with its contents: that was a concept that would have to wait another ten years.

The place had been Hamilton property since medi-aeval times, but the house as it existed in 1919 was principally the work of the 3rd Duke, who died in 1694; the 5th Duke, who came of age in 1724, and the 10th Duke, who married William Beckford's daughter and who succeeded in 1819. At the end of his life the 3rd Duke employed James Smith, who also reconstructed Dalkeith outside Edinburgh, to rebuild the existing house on the site, and it was under his direction that William Morgan and others worked on the richly carved state rooms. The 5th Duke commissioned William Adam to remodel other rooms, and he also built Chatelherault, the shooting lodge in the great park. Recently that structure has been restored, and the principal evidence for the repair of its ceiling was the *Country Life* photograph published on June 14, 1919. The 10th Duke employed David Hamilton to rebuild the north front in 1822-25.

154. *The bedchamber and the enfilade through the state rooms*

155. (Opposite above) *The Duchess's boudoir at Hamilton Palace*

157. (Above) *The heraldic overmantel in the drawing room*

156. (Opposite below) *The canopy and chair of state in the gallery*

Coleshill

Berkshire

It is one of the great English architectural tragedies of the twentieth century that Coleshill was burned in 1953. It was the masterpiece of Sir Roger Pratt, a Norfolk squire and gentleman architect, who designed it for his cousin, Sir George Pratt, soon after he returned to England from six years abroad. Building began in 1649 and was completed in 1662, when Richard Cleare, a well known London craftsman, submitted his account for the carving of the great doorways and the staircase. In 1945 Ernest Cook bought it, with the intention of bequeathing it to the National Trust, but it was gutted when some repairs were being done to the roof. Now all that exists, apart from some gate piers and some eighteenth century overmantels containing Pleydell portraits now at Longford Castle, is the set of *Country Life* photographs taken by A.E. Henson for the articles published in 1919. Tippings articles overturned the traditional attribution to Inigo Jones: 'If we now run through all the available evidence, then will arise the conviction that Inigo Jones certainly had an advisory position, but that, Sir Roger Pratt was the active and acting architect.' It was Tipping who discovered about Sir Roger's involvement at Coleshill, although his notebooks were not published by R.T. Gunther until 1928. Its best epitaph is that by Sir John Summerson: 'Thus, in this remarkable house Pratt combined the fruits of his travel experience with much learnt from Jones and the usual Italian books. Massive, serene, thoughtful, absolutely without affectation, Coleshill was a statement of the utmost value to British architecture.'

158. (Below) *The great staircase in the hall*

159. (Opposite above) *The hall ceiling. We are told that Inigo Jones "was also consulted abt ye Ceilings"*

160. (Opposite below) *The saloon on the first floor*

Wardes

KENT

This fourteenth century yeoman's house was restored about 1912 by Sir Louis Mallet (1864-1936), a diplomat with an unusually good eye who seems to have had a considerable influence on a number of his friends. In 1913-14, when he was Ambassador in Constantinople, he had serving under him Lord Gerald Wellesley, Colonel Reggie Cooper (one of whose houses appears in 190, 191) and Harold Nicolson. Philip Tilden in his memoirs acknowledged his debt to Sir Louis, describing him as 'a man of rare taste and genius. . . . That little house at Otham was probably the most perfectly chosen and arranged set of objects, circumstances and materials that England had to show. Again there was no millionaire's purse, but only flair for collection and a perfect sense of cumulative effect, colour, form.' Tilden in his turn owed a great deal to Sir Louis, whom he met through Martin Conway, and to Sir Philip Sassoon. The photographs of Wardes in *Country Life* were taken shortly before Sir Louis left, and by the time Philip Mainwaring Johnston's article appeared on August 30, 1919, the house had been sold to Lady Juliet Trevor (better known as Lady Juliet Duff).

161. *The fourteenth-century hall*

162 and 163. (Opposite) *The living room. Philip Tilden painted the overmantel*

Beaudesert
STAFFORDSHIRE

To those who think of the Industrial Revolution as being an eighteenth-and nineteenth-century development, it may come as a surprise that the Pagets who were granted Beaudesert in 1546 were mining for coal on their Staffordshire estate in the sixteenth century. By the early twentieth century the Cannock coalfield might have seemed a discouraging place to a landowner, but when a fire took place at Beaudesert in 1909 that gave the 6th Marquess of Anglesey what must have seemed a welcome opportunity. As Tipping wrote in *Country Life* on November 22 and 29, 1919, 'It had suffered excessive-

ly from an outburst of neo-Gothicism a hundred years ago [by Potter of Lichfield who did pretty sub-Wyatt work at Plas Newydd, the Angleseys' other house], and the object was to give back to it, in very large measure, but with some later features and modern conveniences, the character it had possessed towards the close of Elizabeth's reign.' In this Lord Anglesey was assisted by Edmund Warre, who designed a new wing, and by Captain Harry Lindsay, a kinsman of his future wife, an amateur of architecture who helped with the alterations, decoration and furnishing. A new, rather unconvincing Great Hall was formed, and – as a sign of the times – in it was placed a long table found in the servants hall at Holme Lacy and bought for Beaudesert at the sale. The Long Gallery was restored to its original extent and the wainscotting made good, the new work being 'toned

down in the cool grey colour that the old assumed during the process of cleaning off'; the overmantel, the one good Elizabethan feature surviving, was carefully restored, the damaged fireplace that was discovered was copied and the missing frieze was taken from that in the Bromley by Bow Room in the Victoria and Albert Museum (6). Some features were copied from elsewhere, as in the Yellow Drawing Room, which combined details from mid-seventeenth-century work at Forde Abbey and Thorpe Hall. The Queen Anne room was created round old unused Chinese wallpaper found elsewhere by Harry Lindsay, while a state bed was acquired from Hinton St. George. The wallpaper in the state bedroom was original to the house, as was the early eighteenth century bed upholstered in painted silk. The interior was intentionally eclectic: as Tipping wrote, it was 'a remarkably complete and extensive example of the tendency of our age to re-create the past in all matters of architecture and the decorative arts.' However it was short lived, because the house was demolished in 1932.

164. (Opposite) *The new great hall*

165. (Below) *Chinese wallpaper in the State Bedroom*

Houghton Hall

NORFOLK

'Now all smiles once more. Reparations, which in no way interfere with the spirit of the past, make Houghton once more the splendid house where Sir Robert entertained during the late years of his great ministry.' The quotation comes from the series of articles in 1921, which marked the establishment in the house of the late Marquess of Cholmondeley and the present Dowager Marchioness, who had married in 1913 and moved to Houghton in 1919. Although many accounts of the house have been published since then, this set of photographs remains the most extensive record of the state rooms. They stand out as a major statement at the outset of the 1920s of the new-found enthusiasm for grand Early Georgian classicism and, in particular, appreciation of the work of William Kent.

The photograph of the Marble Parlour which shows the chimneypiece and the flanking arches, with one of the side tables that can be reached through the hidden service door, must have appealed to Lutyens, because he copied the idea in the Viceroy's House in Delhi and at Gledstone Hall (see figs. 229, 260).

It is astonishing how little the state rooms have changed during the past sixty-seven years. The most significant alterations have been the enrichment of the contents, particularly in the White Drawing Room, which now contains some of the pictures and French furniture that Lady Cholmondeley inherited from her brother, Sir Philip Sassoon.

166. (Below) *Rysbrack's chimneypiece and overmantel in the Marble Parlour*

167. (Opposite) *The Stone Hall*

168. *The centre window with Kent's pier tables and glasses in the saloon at Houghton*

169. *The White Drawing Room. The silk hangings in a Louis Seize*
style were hung at the end of the eighteenth century

The Beech House, Worthing

Sussex

Although the Beech House only had a short life in the form in which it appeared in *Country Life* on January 29, 1921, it was an important influence at the time, and the photographs remain a valuable record of an early Regency Revival house. It belonged to Edward Knoblock, a Henry Jamesian kind of American – indeed they were friends – who is now best known for having written *Kismet*. He spent a good deal of his early life in France before settling in England, and even before the First World War he was interested in the Directoire and Early Empire styles, furnishing his apartment in The Palais Royal accordingly. In 1914 he took chambers in Albany, and, with the help of Maxwell Ayrton, he decorated those rooms in an English equivalent of the Empire style, 'solemn Regency' as he called it. Towards the end of the War he discovered the Beech House, and also he made some outstanding purchases of Thomas Hope furniture at the Deepdene sale in 1917. Afterwards he called on Maxwell Ayrton to help, and one of the rooms they decorated was the Drawing Room, which was hung with a French landscape wallpaper. He had an American sense of thoroughness in matters of decoration and arrangement, and that, combined with his French experience, meant that the house could never have felt wholly English. However the results were much admired and his later rooms in London can be seen alongside Lord Gerald Wellesley's (see figs. 219, 220, 221).

170. *The inner hall*

171. (Opposite above) *A French landscape wallpaper in the drawing room*

172. (Opposite below) *A bed recess*

Canons Ashby

NORTHAMPTONSHIRE

At the end of the last century Canons Ashby was frequently chosen for illustration in books on historic houses and gardens, partly because it had belonged for sixty-one years to a well known antiquary, Sir Henry Dryden, who encouraged study of it. He inherited in 1837 and died in 1898.

The articles on February 26, March 5 and 12, 1921 by J.A. Gotch, the Northamptonshire architect and antiquarian, record the house in the time of Sir Arthur Dryden, shortly before it began to go into the melancholy decline that was only finally halted and reversed in 1980, when the house was acquired by the National Trust. Its subsequent restoration was greatly helped by the photographs and an earlier set taken in 1904. For example, it was possible to remake the festoon curtains and rehang the portraits high up in the dining room. In 1921 the Tapestry Room still contained the tapestries hung over the windows by Edward Dryden in 1710, the bed made up by Sir Henry, the Antiquary, and the needlework furniture supplied to Edward Dryden in 1716. That was sold after the Second World War, and by an extraordinary chance recovered for the house while it was being restored by the National Trust, when it suddenly and unexpectedly reappeared on the market. The recovery of the furniture would have particularly pleased Margaret Jourdain, who knew the house when she was young because she was a friend of Alice Dryden, the only daughter of Sir Henry. Indeed they shared various interests, and her first book, on lace, was written in collaboration with Alice Dryden. Gotch also illustrated the kitchen, with its big eighteenth-century arch, saying it is 'well worth seeing, and after breakfast, under suitable guidance, the visitor will probably see it.'

173. (Opposite above) *The Tapestry Room*

174. (Opposite below) *The dining room*

175. *The kitchen*

Avebury Manor

WILTSHIRE

Like so many of the manor houses described in *Country Life* before and after the First War, Avebury had declined into being a farm house, although all the old family pictures and furniture remained in the house. Thus when the old tenant farmer died about 1900, it was leased as it stood to Colonel Leopold Jenner. It was presumably through him that Inigo Triggs included a view of its garden gate in his book on formal gardens in 1902. Five years later Colonel Jenner was able to buy the freehold and he and his wife began the restoration of the house and the garden, while his brother Sir Walter, the 2nd baronet, bought Lytes Cary in Somerset, which he left to the National Trust in 1948. The two Jenner

brothers married two sisters and both carried out notable restorations, the Leopold Jenners having exceptional sensitivity and talent when it came to handling an old house. As the author of the articles published on April 30 and May 7, 1921, wrote: 'The study of ancient English life at its best – its architecture, its decoration, its furniture, as well as its pastimes and habits – had been their pleasure': Avebury was as thoroughly suited to them as they were to Avebury. 'A dozen years of thoughtful work and continued occupation have made the manor a singularly complete and satisfying example of a very delightful type of a long existent and much enduring English country house.'

On the ground floor the principal room was the Dining Room, a handsome early Georgian room, which they hung with 'a flock paper imitative of a Genoa cut velvet of the period.' Perhaps the most remarkable achievement was Mrs Jenner's in the Great Chamber. 'It rather called

for one of those tall upholstered beds that prevailed when Anne was Queen. Mrs Jenner, who combines admirable taste in needlework with energetic assiduity in its production, determined, with her needle and the help of a carpenter, to create a specimen founded on the most complete and elaborate needlework examples of the time. To have worked those vast expanses of fine canvas might appear to many a life task. But it was only an incident in the Avebury upholstery undertaken by its chatelaine, to whom are due the coverings of the settees, chairs and stools that appear in the illustrations of the various rooms, except in the case of those places that had preserved their original upholstery.' Of the furniture Tipping wrote that it 'has been long and assiduously collected with the view of being in complete harmony with its surroundings . . . there is no hard and fast rule of allowing nothing later. When that rule is laid down the result is often a little museum-like and unsympathetic.

The true note of homeliness is struck where natural taste and feeling have allowed just enough variety of style and character of piece to give a sense of continuous habitation.' A generation later the approach of the Jenners seemed to have less appeal, as James Lees-Milne records in *Ancestral Voices* in 1942: 'Eardley [Knollys, a National Trust colleague and friend] was bored by the house because it is not classical and is romantic. Today's fashionable distaste for the romantic in English country houses is as over-emphasized as was the Edwardians' for the classical and the regular.'

176. (Opposite) *The Georgian dining room*

177. (Below) *Mrs Jenner's needlework bed in the Great Chamber*

Port Lympne
KENT

Port Lympne was probably the most exotic country house in England between the wars. The original house was commissioned from Herbert Baker by Sir Philip Sassoon, when he became MP for Hythe in 1912. After the War, when he decided to enlarge it, he renamed it Port Lympne and, with the aid of Philip Tilden, gave it a much more imaginative and varied character. As a result the anonymous author of the articles on May 19 and 26, 1923, wrote: 'The rooms at Port Lympne are a compact fairy palace in which one walks, wide-eyed, as though on air.' The dining room was given an Egyptian character through Glyn Philpot's frieze painted in black, chocolate and white, while the walls were the colour of lapis lazuli, the gilt chairs had jade coloured cushions, the carpet was grey and the ceiling opalescent. The drawing room was decorated by Sert with wallpaintings in black and gold, with a gilt ceiling. In contrast to them the small original library designed in the classical style for Sir Philip's own use by Philip Tilden seems almost sober, and to look forward to the more restrained and classical feeling of Trent Park (figs. 225, 226, 227).

The appearance of the house and its gardens was matched by the life described by Robert Boothby in *I Fight to Live* (1947): 'Throughout the strange and often bewildering inter-war period, Sir Philip Sassoon set the stage, with lavish splendour, for a social scene the like of which we shall certainly never see again.'

178. *Sir Philip Sassoon's private library designed by Philip Tilden*

179. (Opposite above) *Egyptian decoration in the dining room by Philpot*

180. (Opposite below) *The drawing room painted by Sert. The subject is* France being Attacked by Germany and Eventually Triumphing

The Queen's Dolls House

When Christopher Hussey wrote about the Dolls House on February 9, 1924, he imagined himself as Defoe on a *Voyage to Lilliput* giving 'a True and Particular Account of my Visite to a Newly Erected Portion of the Imperial Palace of Lilliput, together with some Observations on the Architectural Styles of Furnishing thereof.' Sixty years later the article reads as a rather arch conceit, but in fact the idea came from the official book about the project by A.C. Benson and Sir Lawrence Weaver.

It is more helpful to turn to Hussey's account of it in his *Life of Edwin Lutyens*, which explains its presence in this anthology. It was the kind of house that Lutyens would have built in 1920 but for the effects of the war, when 'taxation rendered virtually impossible resumption of the kind of building to which Lutyens had been accustomed, and very doubtful the survival of the social class and aesthetic standards on which his practice had been built.' The idea of the dolls house was conceived at a dinner party in 1920 'as a tribute by many hands to the affection felt for Her Majesty by the British people' to be exhibited at the 1924 British Empire Exhibition. As A.C. Benson wrote, 'The project could never have been carried out without a presiding genius who had within his powers both efficiency and a keen sense of fun.' And while it came at a moment when Lutyens' private practice was quiet and Delhi was still paralysed by the war, it must have been a much greater undertaking than he could have ever envisaged; and in the end it proved to be his most fully detailed house apart from Delhi. While its principal rooms are a microcosm of historic interiors reinterpreted by Lutyens, the working parts of the house are probably the most complete statement of attitudes and practices at that time, and so an invaluable social document.

Nearly 1,500 people were involved in it, including Gertrude Jekyll who advised on the garden, Percy Macquoid who advised on the furniture and wrote that section of the book, and George Muntzer who usually did upholstery for Lutyens. Among the many subscribers was Edward Hudson, who gave the furniture for the butler's bedroom; he also had a special camera and lenses made for the photography of the interior. The Queen took a deep interest in the progress of her house, and as early as 1921 she told Lutyens that she wanted to be able to open it by herself, without summoning servants, so that she could play with it; and there is a delightful account of her coming with the King to inspect it when it was finished and asking for them to be left on their own with it for half an hour.

181. (Opposite) *The library. The ceiling was painted by William Walcot, and the shelves contain books in MS by famous authors*

182. (Above) *The Queen's bedroom*

183. (Above) *The linen room*   184. (Below) *A housemaid's closet*

185. (Above) *The kitchen*   186. (Below) *The scullery*

Chilham Castle
KENT

The castle close to the Jacobean house that succeeded it was built by Henry II in the 1170s, and all that survives of it is the keep. When it was illustrated in *Country Life* on June 21, 1924, it was the home of Charles Ricketts (1863-1937) the artist and Charles Shannon (1866-1931) the illustrator, who had been given it for life by Sir Edmund Davis, a collector with a South African fortune who had bought Chilham in 1918. As well as being artists, Ricketts and Shannon were life-long collectors, who left most of their possessions to the Fitzwilliam Museum at Cambridge. Some idea of their eclectic taste and eye for striking arrangement can be seen in the photographs. The use of the Indian chintz palampores is particularly imaginative. When they lived in the tower it was thought to be in origin a much older building, Christopher Hussey writing that it was apparently the oldest inhabited building in England, with foundations and some of the walls being 'Roman work directly comparable with the Pharos at Dover.'

187. *Printed fabrics in the guest chamber*

188. (Opposite) *The octagonal hall*

Cold Ashton Manor

GLOUCESTERSHIRE

Today it seems extraordinary that someone of comfortable means, but not vast resources, could move from manor house to manor house restoring them, furnishing them and making gardens so that they became complete works of art. Not only that, but that there were still delightful worthwhile houses asking to be taken on.

When this house was described on February 14 and 21, 1925 by Christopher Hussey, it had belonged to Colonel Reginald Cooper for only a matter of months, but, after being a farm house for two-hundred years, it had 'recaptured with his assistance, the glamour of its youth.' Colonel Cooper, whose touch with old houses was as magical as his enthusiasm was great, became a great friend of Christopher Hussey. He had been in the Diplomatic Service before the First War, serving in Istanbul under Sir Louis Mallet, with Lord Gerald Wellesley and Harold Nicolson, who remained close friends. Like Sir Louis he had a marvellous eye, particularly for mellow textures and for assembling objects, and evidently that was more important to him than the quality of individual pieces. Thus 'Jacobean, late Stuart and Georgian congregate in the fashion of original inhabitants, but, at the same time, neither gives the impression of a collection nor contrives to clutter up the rooms . . . Everything has that natural and untouched appearance that only the most sympathetic restoration can give.' In the Crimson Damask Bedroom, for instance, the walls were hung with a flock paper in crimson and gold, while another was in black and gold. 'This sounds gaudy,' wrote Christopher Hussey, 'but in effect is very mellow.' It was the act of creation that appealed to Colonel Cooper, and once he had finished a house, he soon wanted to start on another; and off he went first to Cothay, in Somerset, then to Julians in Hertfordshire and finally to Knightstone in Devon.

189. *The screen in the hall*

190. (Opposite above) *The Elizabethan hall*

191. (Opposite below) *A velvet bed*

Penheale Manor

CORNWALL

Captain N.R. Colville had a rather different approach to Colonel Cooper in that he was a connoisseur with an exceptional eye for works of art, in particular Old Master drawings and English furniture; his perfectionism extended to the great care he took over the framing of drawings in fine old frames and protecting them from light with fragments of old silk and velvet.

As a result of being gassed in the First World War he was advised to move south from Scotland, and it was then that he found the almost ruinous old manor house at Penheale, which he repaired and commissioned Lutyens to enlarge, adding on at the back a tower house at the same time as Drogo was rising. The relationship between the old house and the new building is so skilfully handled that the new is never allowed to intrude

on the old. Captain Colville restored the interior, including re-opening the Gallery, made to show off his English furniture, which included a number of pieces with their original upholstery. That the 1925 articles were written by Ralph Edwards show how important the collecting of English furniture was at that time. Indeed without such collectors it would never have been possible to compile the *Dictionary*, while equally without the photographic resources of the magazine it would never have been possible to gather the illustrations together. The illustrations shown here were not reproduced in the articles, and changes of detail in the arrangement of the hall and dining room suggest that Captain Colville probably objected to what was depicted, and asked for some of the photographs to be retaken. The view of the Hall, for instance, corresponds with one published but not the other, while the Dining Parlour was shown with the table not laid and the lampshades removed from the chandelier. Today the luxury of such changes of mind could not be afforded.

192. *The hall with its carved screen set up between 1637 and 1644*

193. (Opposite below) *The panelled dining room*

194. (Opposite above) *Notable English furniture in the gallery*

Brocket Hall

HERTFORDSHIRE

The saloon is the climax to the house designed about 1765 by James Paine for Sir Matthew Lamb, and completed for his son, Sir Peniston, who was created Lord Melbourne in 1770, the year of his marriage. The room was not finally completed until Wheatley took over the painting of the ceiling after the death of Mortimer in 1779. This photograph was taken in 1923 before Brocket was sold to Sir Charles Nall-Cain, later 1st Lord Brocket, and was first published on July 18, 1925. Sir Charles bought the carpets, the pier glasses, tables, pelmet cornices, chandelier and the great Reynolds of the Prince of Wales given by the Prince to Lady Melbourne. But sadly, the splendid hangings were not included, and all trace of them has been lost.

195. *The saloon. The hangings were probably lampas, what contemporaries called a three-colour damask*

Heveningham Hall

SUFFOLK

This is one of the well known *Country Life* photographs of one of the finest of all James Wyatt's interiors, and was first illustrated on September 19, 1925. It is chosen because it reveals one of the tricks that photographers of the time got up to. The scagliola floor appears to have a very high polish to it, which was apparently achieved by photographing it wet. The Vannecks acquired Heveningham in 1752, and in 1777 Sir Gerard, the second baronet, consulted Sir Robert Taylor about a remodelling of the house, but how and exactly when Taylor was superseded by Wyatt is not known, although it is evident that the hall was finished by 1784, when a Frenchman, François de la Rochefoucauld, describes staying there.

196. *The entrance hall. The appearance of a high polish on the floor was achieved by keeping it wet*

Westwood Manor

WILTSHIRE

'Each time I come here I am overwhelmed by the perfection of this house. Everything Ted has done to it is in the best possible taste and proves his astonishing, instructive understanding of the late mediaeval and Jacobean periods.' So wrote James Lees-Milne in *Ancestral Voices*, his diary for 1942.

At the time E.G. Lister was trying to decide what should happen to the house after his death, and was discussing with James Lees-Milne its possible devise to the National Trust. He had bought the house, which had been a farm house, in 1911, while still serving in the Diplomatic Service, and began its careful restoration. Most unusually, he was allowed to write about the place in *Country Life* in 1926. A medieval, Tudor and Jacobean manor house that forms a romantic group with the church, it had declined into being a farmhouse in the eighteenth century and then in the early nineteenth century it aroused the curiosity of antiquarians like J.C. Buckler. He described how the Great Parlour, which had been formed in the upper part of the Great Hall in the early seventeenth century, had been divided into two and its chimney piece had been all but completely destroyed. The present fireplace and the four arcaded panels above were an exceedingly skilful restoration, with but the scantiest material for a guide, by Mr Smallcorn of Bath. In the King's Room it was he who installed the panelling and also the series of portraits of sovereigns that he had obtained from Keevil Manor in 1910. The house passed to the National Trust on his death in 1956.

197. (Opposite) *The great parlour*

198. (Below) *The Kings Room*

Castle Howard

YORKSHIRE

A set of 140 photographs were taken in 1924 when Tipping and Hussey were gathering material for their Vanbrugh volume of *English Homes*, which finally appeared in 1928; and Tipping published them in five long articles in June 1927. They show the brilliance of A.E. Henson's work and they were to prove an invaluable record, because when the house was seriously damaged by fire in 1940, the dome was burned and some interiors were completely lost. When the late

George Howard decided to restore the dome in 1961-62, not only were the *Country Life* negatives produced but Mr Henson, by then retired, was able to produce his lens, so it was possible to take precise measurements for a restoration based on photogrametry, the details of which were published in *The Photogrametric Record* (see page 9).

Apparently Henson had made himself thoroughly unpopular with the staff, because he insisted that the floor of the Mausoleum should be cleared of a generous coating of bird droppings before being polished for him, and that servants should be on hand to keep it wet while he took his photograph.

199. *Classical sculpture in a corridor*

200. (Opposite) *The central hall*

Snowshill Manor

GLOUCESTERSHIRE

Snowshill is the strange, dream-like, creation of Charles Wade, an architect with ample private means who in about 1900 began to collect everyday artefacts of the previous 200 years. In 1919 he acquired the property of Snowshill in a dilapidated state. Over the years he filled the main building with a bizarre mixture of objects artfully arranged, so that a nostaligic feeling for the past is combined with a sense of theatre. He himself lived in an adjoining building, 'refusing electric light, eating in an old world kitchen, sleeping in an old world Tudor cupboard-bed, working at self appointed tasks with period tools in a reconstructed forge and workshop,' as H.D. Molesworth wrote in the National Trust guidebook in 1965.

The *Country Life* article on October 1, 1927, was written by A.E. Richardson, a choice of author that is revealing in itself, because, while the mood was very different from that of Avenue House (figs. 257, 258, 259), both men liked to live in a world of their imagination and found reality in simple relics of the past. In fact they were old friends, as Simon Houfe explained in his memoir of his grandfather, and they found their houses about the same time: 'They had entered architecture at about the same time, and their passionate interest in craftsmanship and the past had drawn them together.' He recalled visits there with his grandfather in the 1950s and 60s: 'There was always the smell of wood smoke at Snowshill, burning oak or apple in the hot ash, pervading the whole house even in summer and mixing with the odours of drying pomanders and old faded stuffs. Lavender or orange-blossom scents might seep through an open door for an instant but were soon overcome by the all-embracing smells of age.' The 1927 photographs show a much more conventional arrangement than that existing by the time Charles Wade gave the house to the National Trust in 1951, five years before his death.

201. (Below) *Architect's corner. Part of Charles Wade's Lodging*

202. (Opposite above) *The dining room*

203. (Opposite below) *The smoking room*

Beningbrough

YORKSHIRE

Beningbrough in the years after 1917 was an admirable example of the intelligent taste of that time. That year it was bought by the Earl of Chesterfield, allegedly to please his wife, who came from Yorkshire; but it was a good choice, because it was not so different in character from his former home, Holme Lacy in Herefordshire (figs. 110, 111, 112), which he had sold some years earlier. Wisely he had kept not only the late seventeenth and early eighteenth-century furniture but also the Grinling Gibbons carvings, which suited Beningbrough with its fine complementary carving by the York school. Indeed it now emerges that Beningbrough was designed by William Thornton of York, a carpenter and carver by trade, who had worked at Castle Howard and seems to have gone on to Wentworth Castle from Beningbrough, when the latter was completed about 1716. The house was illustrated in *Country Life* (for

the second time) on November 25 and December 3, 1927, when work on the Vanbrugh volume of *English Homes* was in course of preparation. The illustrations suggest that the house and the contents were made to pull together in a harmonious way that was strongly influenced by the style of Lenygon and Morant. After the death of Lady Chesterfield the house was offered to the Treasury in settlement of estate duty, and transferred to the National Trust in 1958, but, unfortunately, only part of the contents was acquired, so undermining the unity and leaving it rather bare. As a result many of the colours and finishes no longer worked, but even so the unhistorical stripped woodwork has been retained in the drawing room, because it represents the taste of the Chesterfields' time.

204. (Below) *The drawing room. The woodwork had been recently stripped in accordance with current fashion*

205. (Opposite) *Portraits and carving from Holme Lacy in the hall*

Dorchester House

LONDON

It was described by Christopher Hussey in his articles on May 6 and 12, 1928 as 'a private palace of monumental construction and unusual beauty on one of the most pictorial sites in London.' The house had been designed by Lewis Vulliamy for R.S. Holford and built between 1848 and 1863, and at the time of the articles it was about to be demolished. Its sale, together with that of the Holford collection of pictures and of Westonbirt, had followed the death of Sir George Holford, but considerable efforts were made to save the building. The Italian Government considered it for their embassy, while Lady Beecham wanted to use it to house a national opera; but neither could raise the necessary money. Christopher Hussey's obituary is written in considerably stronger language than Tipping's on Hamilton Palace nine years earlier: 'A country that lives on capital, treating death duties as income, must not expect monuments of individualism to survive.' It is interesting that he saw its building as spanning the years that marked the change of mood in the nineteenth century: its conception came at 'the high-water mark of aristocracy in the nineteenth century. When it was begun London Society had never been more brilliant and international, with a queen still young, whose consort had contrived to add to the wealth and surviving splendour of late Georgian society nobility of ideals.' But then had come the Crimean War, the Indian Mutiny and the death of the Prince Consort, and before Dorchester House was finished 'the society that was to grace it had lost its lustre.'

Among many splendours, the most important and tantalising room was the dining room on which Alfred Stevens worked from 1859 until his death in 1875, when it was still unfinished. Even so, Christopher Hussey considered his carved and sculptural decorations as 'the chief example of the work of perhaps the greatest English artist.'

206. (Opposite) *The staircase hall*

207. (Below) *Alfred Steven's dining room*

Blickling Hall

NORFOLK

Blickling was the first great country house and estate to come to the National Trust under the Country Houses Scheme, in 1940, and it was bequeathed by the 11th Marquess of Lothian, whose speech to the Annual General Meeting of the National Trust in 1934 had led to the Trust formulating its scheme. It is interesting to speculate on the extent to which Lord Lothian's thinking was influenced by his own experience on inheriting Blickling in 1930 from his cousin. Not only was he faced by death duties, but the house had been let before he succeeded, and in 1930 it was let again.

The house was described by Christopher Hussey in *Country Life* on June 7, 21 and 28, 1930, and, although he does not touch on any current problems, or its future, it needs to be related to leaders in *Country Life* in the late 1930s and early 1930s and to Lord Lothian's speech, which seems to cover some of the same ground.

Nearly sixty years later the most interesting section of the articles is that on the Gallery, whose decoration was planned in 1858 by J.H. Pollen, 'at once the glory and the pity of Blickling. . . . One's first impression, however, is one of dismay, for under the influence of Mr Ruskin, an attempt was made to give this glorious Jacobean gallery an Early Florentine appearance. The walls are lined with unstained oak bookcases of aggressive shapes, and the dado above them is painted with interlacing designs in crude colour for which it is difficult to adduce a parallel. . . . Of their kind, the decorations are good. In a library in north Oxford, they would look very good. . . . The whole transaction is significant not only of the dogmatism of the Gothic Revival, but of the rise of the cult of "antiques" which developed out of it.'

Given that view, it is perhaps not surprising that Lord Lothian had the huge canopied fireplace removed and the painted decoration over the bookcases obliterated, with the result that the room now feels somewhat watered down, despite its splendid Jacobean ceiling and the quality of the library itself.

Beyond the Gallery the 2nd Earl of Buckinghamshire, in the 1770s, formed two new great rooms, the second of which is the richly decorated State Bedroom with its bed made out of two of the canopies that were perquisites of office as an ambassador.

208. (Opposite) *The gallery. The chimneypiece was subsequently removed and the decoration over the bookcases painted out*

209. (Above) *The State Bedroom. The room was formed to take the bed made out of Lord Buckinghamshire's ambassadorial canopies*

Sir William Orpens' Studio

LONDON

The article by Christopher Hussey in 1930 was prompted by the recent remodelling of the studio at 8 Bolton Gardens by Forbes and Tate, and in it he wrote with perspicacity on the relationship of a portrait painter and his sitters, wishing that he could be painted by Orpen. He went on to describe how 'just beyond the painting chair, so that he can see it in the same glance as he looks at his subject, there was hanging a Manet river scene – sunlight vibrating on water and through thin willow leaves. Although remodelled, it was a building with interesting associations, because Orpen had used the east end for some twenty-five years and in the first decade of that period, Sir Hugh Lane had lived on the ground floor of the west end and had his pictures there, with Shannon in the west studio. Consequently it was appropriate to reproduce Orpen's *Homage to Manet* with that artist's picture of Eva Gonzales that had belonged to Lane and is now in the Tate Gallery.

210. *The sitter's dressing room*

211 and 212. (Opposite) *The Studio. "As he paints, the current in him crackles and sparks as it makes contact with the personality of his sitter."*

Southill

BEDFORDSHIRE

So often old volumes of *Country Life* are referred to for their photographs rather than for their texts, and it tends to be forgotten when articles appeared and why. That comes to mind particularly with Southill, because the *Country Life* set of photographs published on July 12, 19 and 26, 1930 is the standard one. At that time Holland's work carried out for Samuel Whitbread the younger in 1796–1803 was admired for what it was in itself, while at the same time its spare elegance was seen to have a particular relevance to contemporary interior design. Here it has to be remembered that the original upholstery had been simplified and lightened in colour: in the drawing room, for instance, the walls were originally hung with crimson damask bordered in green while the curtains were of red sarsnet with draperies of green velvet. Yet

it is hard to believe that ten years earlier Christopher Hussey wrote; 'Southill must be acknowledged the classic example of the most civilised decade in the whole range of English architecture'; or that the introduction to the third article runs: 'The rooms described are, perhaps, the most exquisite examples of Regency decoration in existence.' Nearly thirty years later, in the Late Georgian volume of his trilogy, Christopher Hussey wrote: 'Architecture and decoration together comprise the most perfect surviving instance of his synthesis of Grecian and French refinements, both with the older classical tradition and English tendencies to empiricism and reticence – the latter strongly represented by the puritanical strain in Whitbread himself.'

213. (Below) *The drawing room.*

214. (Opposite) *The pelmet cornices and draperies in the drawing room*

Wardour Castle

WILTSHIRE

Country Life photographers were never hesitant about playing up the scale and grandeur of an interior, and, when considering the splendid photographs of the staircase at Wardour published on November 22, 1930, it is hard not to feel the influence of paintings of the Pantheon both on the architect and the photographer. The classical house at Wardour was built by the 8th Lord Arundell, largely thanks to the fortunes inherited by his mother and his wife, both of whom were heiresses; and it was one of a number of important commissions that Paine received from leading Catholic landowners. Building was begun in 1768, but it was twenty years before the finest of all Catholic chapels in country houses was finally completed by Soane. As originally at Holkham, there is a surprisingly modest main door, leading into a low Doric entrance hall, with an arch through to the staircase hall, which bursts on visitors, so providing an experience almost as thrilling and unexpected as the great apsed hall at Holkham. The semi-circular flights with their wrought brass balustrades lead round and up to the gallery on the level of the piano nobile where a ring of eight columns carries the dome. There are five exedra behind the ring of columns, with doors inset in four of them and the fifth providing the entrance to the great dining room over the entrance hall.

215. (Below) *The foot of the staircase*

216. (Opposite) *The staircase at first-floor level*

Balmanno Castle

PERTHSHIRE

This was the last of Sir Robert Lorimer's restorations of old Scottish tower houses and castles, and he used to say that it was the most successful, as well as the one that he would like to live in. It was described by Christopher Hussey on March 21 and 28, 1931, two years after the architect's death and at the time when he was completing his memorial volume on him. So the articles contain Hussey's considered view of him as 'perhaps the greatest exponent of Scottish architecture.' ... 'Robert Lorimer succeeded in raising ... a new national tradition of architecture, rooted in the past but expressing the spirit of modern Scotland, and ministered to by a band of craftsmen inspired by his enthusiasm.' He taught them the technique of Scottish craftsmen of the past – masons and joiners, smiths and plasterers – and used his knowledge to express the conceptions of his own time. 'In all his restorations, . . . Lorimer had the rare faculty of renewing the original character of an old building and yet charging it with his own personality, so that, while he made it his own, the work retained its proper individuality.' Also he is careful to record the names of those involved, among them Nathaniel Grieve, who made the oak panelling in the Drawing Room, and Sam Wilson, who did the decorative plasterwork. Lorimer's client was a Glasgow shipowner, William S. Miller, who had bought the place in 1916 when it was still a farmhouse, and the work of restoration and addition was done in 1916-21.

217. (Below) *The old kitchen, adapted as the dining room*

218. (Opposite) *A bedroom at the top of the tower*

11 Montagu Place and 11 Titchfield Terrace, London

These interiors come from an article on 'Four Regency Houses in London' published on April 11, 1931, which is a period piece in a number of ways. It is, for example, surprising now to read that 'there is felt to be something "daring" about having a taste for the Regency period, something that makes friends murmur "how exciting", or raise their eyebrows slightly.' Also it shows the development of the serious interest in Regency furniture and decoration that is particularly associated with Edward Knoblock. By then he was living in Montagu Place (his earlier house, The Beech House at Worthing, had been published in 1921 – see figs. 170, 171, 172) and Lord Gerald Wellesley, a practising architect, was living in Titchfield Terrace. Lord Gerald had been a friend of Christopher Hussey for a number of years, and in fact

they shared a weekend house near West Wycombe. The article also discussed 'the kinship between Regency and modern taste (the product of similar social conditions)', and it showed the influence of the Regency on contemporary work in the house of Goodhart Rendel in Crawford Street and the development of a new simplified classicism in a new house by Lord Gerald that was felt to be a synthesis of traditional and modern design. At the same time the article demonstrated Christopher Hussey's own personal concern with that problem and *Country Life's* awareness of the new interest in interior decoration.

219. (Below) *The drawing room at 11 Montagu Place*

220. (Opposite above) *The drawing room at 11 Titchfield Terrace*

221. (Opposite below) *The dining room at 11 Titchfield Terrace*

High and Over
BUCKINGHAMSHIRE

In the late 1920s and early 1930s Christopher Hussey was seeking to forge a link between modern architecture and traditional styles, and when he wrote about High and Over on September 19, 1931, he was full of enthusiasm: 'This house is the conception of young men, and of young men educated in the classic tradition. . . . Here is architecture pure and unalloyed by sentiment, reminiscence or clap trap. One goes away exhilarated as by a fresh and fertile mind as by the consummate simplicity of a Greek vase.'

Professor Bernard Ashmole, who commissioned it, was Yates Professor of Classical Archaeology at London University and he had met Amyas Connell, his architect, at the British School in Rome.

However, Christopher Hussey was also very much aware of the problem of the relationship of the new architecture to landscape and the need to use materials with sympathy. In discussing the relationship of the house to its setting and the effect of the Town and Planning Bill, he wrote 'every sincere experiment in architecture is to be encouraged, should not be hampered by restrictions that are fundamentally narrow-minded.'

222. *The living room. Jade green cellulose and chromium steel.*

223. (Opposite above) *The cult of fresh air. The roof and day nursery*

224. (Opposite below) *The hexagonal hall*

Trent Park

HERTFORDSHIRE

This was one of the most successful statements of the Georgian enthusiasm of the mid and late 1920s, not only in architectural terms but also in the quality and arrangement of its contents. Sir Philip Sassoon had bought the place in 1923, because of the beauty of Repton's landscape, but the Victorian house, however, proved defeating; and he embarked on a complete remodelling that was illustrated in *Country Life* in 1931.

Christopher Hussey clearly admired what was done: 'Its designer aimed at representing the spirit of English domestic architecture instead of inventing or imitating a specific style. The result is a building at once traditional and modern.'

Sir Philip had a marvellous eye that ranged from the exotic and fanciful to the understated aspects of the English eighteenth-century. He preferred conversation pictures to the grand full length portraits, and japanned and painted furniture to richly carved mahogany or inlaid satinwood. Thus the simplification of his taste in the 1920s ran parallel to the simplification of classicism.

The house formed the setting for a way of life vividly described by Robert Boothby in *I Fight to Live* (1947): 'His hospitality was on an oriental scale. The summer week-end parties at Trent were unique and in the highest degree enjoyable, but theatrical rather than intimate. . . . Today it all seems like a dream of another world – the white-coated footmen serving endless courses of rich but delicious food, the Duke of York coming in from golf, an immaculate Sir Samuel Hoare playing tennis with the professional, Winston Churchill arguing over the tea-cups with Bernard Shaw, Lord Balfour dozing in an arm chair, Rex Whistler absorbed in his painting, Osbert Sitwell and Malcolm Bullock laughing in a corner, while Philip himself flitted from group to group, an alert, watchful, influential, but unobtrusive stage director – all set against a background of mingled luxury, simplicity, and informality, brilliantly contrived . . .'

225. *The dining room. The architect's name was not given in the article, presumably at the request of Sir Philip Sassoon*

226. (Opposite above) *The Venetian window in the drawing room*

227. (Opposite below) *A bedroom*

Viceroy's House, Delhi
INDIA

In its first thirty-eight years *Country Life* illustrated many castles, houses, palaces and gardens abroad, but its most ambitious venture, which must have been Edward Hudson's idea, was to send the photographer Arthur Gill to Delhi in 1931 to record the completion of the new Imperial capital. Lutyens invited his old friend to accompany him and they stayed in the Viceroy's House. It must have been one of the crowning experiences of Hudson's life, the culmination of over thirty years of support and encouragement; but characteristically he is not known to have written any account of his impressions. The series of five articles covering thirty-five pages were written by Robert Byron, who also wrote a com-

plementary series for *The Architectural Review*. Byron was evidently thrilled and moved by 'the greatness of this last of the great palaces,' as he wrote in his second article on the interior. His third article was devoted to the Decorations of the House: 'Few palace interiors have exhibited such pomp of form and decoration. And never before has this outmoded virtue achieved such unanimity with domestic convenience. An individual and peculiarly English splendour pervades the rooms and corridors, a splendour which, far from continuing the immemorial tradition of Royal vulgarity, expresses, perhaps for the last time, the spirit of humanist aristocracy in the language of a dwelling.' Looking at the illustrations of the rooms, it seems possible to sense Lutyens' distillation of ideas seen in *Country Life*; echoes of St Stephens Walbrook in the State Library, of Blenheim and Castle Howard in its corridors, and of Houghton in the Semi-State Dining Room.

228. *The main vestibule within the portico*

229. (Opposite above) *The Semi-State Dining Room*

230. (Opposite below) *The State Library*

Berkeley Castle

GLOUCESTERSHIRE

The articles published in 1932, which were the result of *Country Life's* second visit, record the restoration and alterations carried out over the previous decade by the 8th (and last) Earl of Berkeley, who was born in 1865, succeeded in 1888 and died in 1942. The lineal descendant in the male line of the builder of the castle in the mid twelfth century, he was deeply interested in its history and concerned to solve the riddles presented by its fabric. At the same time there is a certain freedom and lavishness of approach that might suggest an American touch, and it is interesting that in 1924 Lord Berkeley married, as his second wife, Mary Emlen Lloyd, the daughter of John Dowell of Boston. Fittings were removed or taken to other parts of the castle, while others were brought in from elsewhere. In the Great Hall formed in the middle of the fourteenth century, for instance, Lord Berkeley removed 'dark Victorian panelling and other poor fittings that obscured its form' and installed the sixteenth-century screen from Caefn Mably in Pembrokeshire, repainting the Kemys black and white chevrons in the Berkeley red and white. The Chapel was made into a drawing room and the mid fifteenth century gallery introduced at the dissolution of the monasteries was moved next door to the new Great Drawing Room. The alterations were done by Keebles, who were architectural decorators.

231. *The great drawing room with its gothic gallery*   232. (Opposite) *The fourteenth-century Great Hall*

233. *Walter Tapper's Great Hall*

234. (Opposite) *The garden Hall. It survived the fire in 1947*

Nymans

SUSSEX

Nymans is one of the best illustrations of the effect of the passion for gardening and plants that developed in the years round 1900, and the way it has continued to influence taste and attitudes. In 1890 the place was acquired by Ludwig Messel, because it was not only within easy reach of London but also provided a marvellous opportunity for garden-making on green sand.

In 1915 he was succeeded by his son, Colonel Leonard Messel, who was married to Maude Sambourne, the daughter of Linley Sambourne, whose house in Stafford Terrace, Kensington, is one of the most remarkable surviving examples of artistic Victorian taste. Colonel Messel was a considerable collector as well as a gardener, and his wife shared his enthusiasms and was also a talented artist. If they had not inherited Nymans with its special qualities as a garden, they would have looked for a mediaeval or Tudor manor house in the West Country, like Cothay or Westwood. As it was they decided to stay and to transform the existing undistinguished house into a romantic evocation of a manor house, employing in succession Walter Tapper and Norman Evill to help them, with the latter working on sketches provided by Mrs Messel.

Christopher Hussey, who wrote about Nymans on September 10 and 17, 1932, said: 'So clever a reproduction is it of a building begun in the fourteenth century and added to intermittently till Tudor times, that some future antiquary may well be deceived by it, even if not inspired to elaborate a correspondingly convincing history.' Indeed under the pseudonym of Curious Crowe that he invented for himself for use in *Country Life*, he wrote just such an outline history that is a mixture of fact, fantasy and teasing. It is extraordinary to find him not only seeing the point of what the Messels had done, but obviously enjoying it, only a year after he wrote about High and Over. Indeed his breadth of approach may explain a great deal: while the Modernists only saw their own way, he believed that there were alternatives dictated by use and situation. Sadly the greater part of the house was gutted by fire in 1947, leaving a ruin that forms an even more romantic feature of the gardens that Colonel Messel left to the National Trust in 1953.

Home House, Portman Square
LONDON

The particular point of the set of *Country Life* photographs is that they show Samuel Courtauld's French pictures as he arranged them. The photographs were taken at the end of his occupation of the house and shortly before his gift to the University was completed. From 1920 to 1926 the house had been occupied by Lord Islington, and in 1927 the lease was taken over by Samuel Courtauld, who carried out a careful restoration on the basis of the original Adam drawings. He endowed the Institute that now bears his name in 1931 and, after his wife died later that year, he decided to give the Portman Square house to it. In the catalogue of *The Courtauld Collection* (1954) Anthony Blunt wrote an essay on 'Samuel Courtauld as Collector and Benefactor' that tells the story. Born in 1876, he entered the family business,

which he greatly expanded during and after the First War. Long before, however, he had become interested in painting. He began to appreciate Degas on his first visit to Paris, but the real turning point was going to Florence and Rome in 1901, soon after his marriage. 'The old masters had come alive for me, and British academic art had died.' Later he became increasingly interested in modern painting, feeling that British painting had come to an end with Turner and Constable. 'My second real "eye opener" was the Hugh Lane collection which was exhibited in London at the Tate Gallery in 1917. There I remember especially Renoir's Parapluies, Manet's Musique des Tuileries and Degas's Plage à Trouville . . . I knew nothing yet of Cezanne.' Samuel Courtauld discovered him at the Burlington Fine Arts Club exhibition in 1922. The following year he gave the Tate Gallery £50,000 to buy nineteenth century French pictures. His own collecting occurred mainly between 1924 and 1929. He died in 1947.

235. *Pictures by Cezanne, Manet and Renoir in the dining room*

236. (Opposite above) *The front drawing room. Over of the fireplace hangs Monet's* Argenteuil *and on the far wall Renoir's* La Loge. 237. (Opposite below) *Impressionist pictures in the front parlour.*

42 Cheyne Walk

LONDON

This was almost a country house in Chelsea, designed by Lutyens for Mr and Mrs G.M. Liddell, and contrary to the usual practice, the Day Nursery (reproduced from a copy negative) and the Servants Hall were illustrated as prominently as the main rooms, in Christopher Hussey's articles on January 14 and 21, 1933. The Servants Hall was decorated with a collection of travel posters, which were made into an orderly scheme through the use of black as a frame on the skirting and cornice and the fireplace, the architect being keen on the use of black in decoration: 'As a form of decoration it is cheap and – for a servants hall, which is usually ornamented at most by pictures long ago (and justly) expelled from spare bedrooms – very humane.' The walls of the Day Nursery were hung with a reprint of an old French landscape paper: 'It would be difficult to devise a more thrilling setting for childhood.' The wallpaper is a particularly good illustration of Lutyens' ability to stimulate and his enjoyment in responding to the imagination of children.

238. (Opposite) *The day nursery, with one of Lutyens's light fittings*

239. (Opposite) *Travel posters in the servants hall*

240. (Right) *The service corridor lined with varnished copies of* The Times

Plumpton Place
Sussex

This was the last of Edward Hudson's country houses and also the last commission that he gave to Edwin Lutyens. As with Deanery Garden, it was the challenge of the site and the possibility of making a garden that had attracted Hudson, and, as soon as he acquired the place in 1928, he began work on the setting of the old Manor House, clearing the lakes and installing cascades as well as converting the Mill House as a simple week-end cottage for his own use. Plans for the Manor House were drawn up, and, although the house was put in order,

alterations – including the addition of a Music Room – were delayed until after the place was described in *Country Life* on May 20, 1933. Lutyens' main architectural contribution was to design an elaborate new approach and entrance consisting of gate piers leading to a pair of cottages laid out as a hollow E forming a gatehouse, with a simple, unaccented, central doorway leading through to a Venetian archway. That faced the new bridge across the water to the island and the main house. The rooms in the Mill House were charmingly furnished with simple but highly desirable eighteenth-century furniture, and suggest how Hudson's own taste had continued to move forward, in the process confirming the impression of the excellence of his eye.

241. *The view from the Mill House across the lake to the Manor House*

242 and 243. (Opposite) *The living room of the Mill House*

Buxted Park

SUSSEX

It is the acquisition, decoration and furnishing of large Georgian houses such as Buxted in the late 1920s and early 1930s that confirm the revival of interest in the eighteenth century and the move on from gables, oak and walnut to porticoes, mahogany and satinwood. Buxted was bought by Mr and Mrs Basil Ionides in 1931, the year after their marriage. He was an architect and decorator who collected Chinese porcelain, and she was a collector of Battersea enamels and eighteenth-century English furniture. Her father was the 1st Lord Bearsted and her first husband was Major W.H. Levy, who had died in 1923. She was introduced to Basil Ionides by Margaret Jourdain, who had been advising her on her collecting since 1922 and was a frequent guest in her London house. Her daughter, Violet Henriques, described Margaret Jourdain to Hilary Spurling as 'a jolly schoolmistress, frightfully dowdy, hair in a little cow pat – part of the family. A nice old bun.'

By the time the articles appeared on April 21 and 28, 1934 work on the house was finished, and it had been made into the acme of elegant comfort, with pretty bedrooms and ingeniously disguised plumbing that was considered particularly worthy of readers' attention. Also they had old wallpaper designs copied, which at that time was thought an original thing to do in England. Sadly, the house was gutted by fire in 1940, and its rebuilding, refitting and refurnishing was one of the few spectacular jobs of its kind done in the 1940s. It made a great impression when it was photographed again for articles published in 1950.

244. *The hall. The arms survived the fire in 1940, but the height of the room was reduced to a single storey*

245. (Opposite) *Yellow scagliola columns in the library*

Nether Lypiatt Manor

GLOUCESTERSHIRE

The catholicity of taste in the houses illustrated in *Country Life* between the wars is remarkable, and, while it says a good deal for the breadth of interest of Tipping and Hussey, it shows what a rich diversity of possibilities there were at that time. Within a few weeks writers could leap from the Long Island splendours of North Mymms to the mellow, understated atmosphere and distinction of Nether Lypiatt, which belonged to Mr and Mrs Gordon Woodhouse, when it was illustrated in *Country Life* on May 19 and 26, 1934. Of its atmosphere at that time there is a vivid record in Osbert Sitwells' *Noble Essences* (1950). Arnold Dolmetsch had persuaded Mrs Woodhouse to take up the harpsichord and clavichord instead of the piano, and Sir Osbert

described how, when he was staying at Nether Lypiatt, 'one morning I happened to be sitting in a corner of the drawing room, when Violet came down. Fortunately, she had not observed me. She opened the harpsichord, raised the top of it, lifting it open, pegged it – all this time I stood motionless – and proceeded to sit down and practise. So intent was she on the job before her, that of phrasing and rephrasing a fugue of Bach's over and over again, that I was able to remain, enthralled, in the room for over an hour while she engaged in an astounding personal contest . . . '

Like so many Cotswold manor houses, Nether Lypiatt had become a farmhouse by the late nineteenth century, and then it was bought for restoration. In 1923, Mr and Mrs Woodhouse saw two short articles on the house in *Country Life* describing the restoration then being carried out for Mr Corbett Woodall by Morley Horder, bought it, and completed the restoration.

246. (Below) *A cabinet in the drawing room*

247. (Below right) *An unusual wardrobe of Nelson chintz*

248. (Opposite above) *Musical instruments in the drawing room*

249. (Opposite below) *The entrance hall*

Wentworth Woodhouse

YORKSHIRE

This photograph, published on September 8, 1934, entitled 'Sporting Pictures in the Billiard Room', is more than a nice piece of under-statement: it shows how such pictures were generally regarded in the late eighteenth century, when owners took a hierarchical view of their houses, their furnishing and arrangement and of the levels of art. Only very rarely, as in the case of Stubbs' 'Whistle Jacket', which gave its name to the former dining room at Wentworth Woodhouse, were sporting pictures considered as state room pictures; generally they were hung in the rooms in daily use, where, incidentally they were seen and enjoyed more by their owners. This group comissioned by the 2nd Marquess of Rockingham, who completed the great house, and by his nephew, the 4th Earl Fitzwilliam, who succeeded him in 1782, is shown hanging against a late eighteenth-century wallpaper similar to the one in the manner of Reveillon in the dining room.

250. (Opposite)
Sporting pictures in the billiards room

251. (Opposite) *The Whistlejacket Room. It was called after Stubbs's painting*

252. (Right) *The great hall. First conceived in the 1730s, but was only completed about 1770*

Joldwynds

SURREY

This house, designed by Oliver Hill and built in 1930-32, makes enthusiasts of Victorian houses particularly cross, because it replaced one by Philip Webb. As Christopher Hussey wrote on September 15, 1934: 'If there may be some disposed to regret the destruction of a building that was just beginning to acquire archaeological and sentimental value, they were probably not considering living in it.' He was full of enthusiasm for the new house: 'A very interesting attempt has been made to design a modern home with beauty. That is to say, to modify the stark utilitarian factors inherent in modern structure in accordance with certain ingrained preferences of the human eye' . . . 'No contemporary architect is better fitted to attempt to warm up the intellectual conception of modern structure in sensuous life.' However, despite its modern appearance it was structurally traditional, being of brick and then rendered in white cement and carborundum, electrically polished to give a surface resembling marble – and, what is more, it gave a great deal of trouble. Among the rooms illustrated (from copy negatives) were the Living Room, which had textiles woven by Marion Dorn and pictures by Ivan Hitchens, and the Dining Room. 'The room is all white – composition floor and combed plaster, the furniture veneered with ivory-coloured shagreen and upholstered in white calf. At the service end an arrangement curiously reminiscent of the mediaeval screen conceals the service entrance and serving table. . . . The whole feature is given character by a rectangular framing in exaggerated perspective.'

253. (Below left) *The stairs at night*

254. (Below) *The view out of the door*

255. (Opposite above) *The sitting room*

256. (Opposite below) *The dining room*

Avenue House, Ampthill

BEDFORDSHIRE

Professor A.E. Richardson's house was one of the few to be described on two occasions between the two wars, first on December 2, 1922, when he had been living there for about three years, and R. Randall Phillips wrote about it in a short article as 'A Lesser Country House of the XVIII century', and then in the main series on December 8, 1934. The Professor had discovered late eighteenth and early nineteenth-century furniture and objects well before the First War, when he chose to live in St Albans because of its eighteenth-century houses. Even then he took great pleasure both in the use of objects and their study, and every year he used to give a Trafalgar Day dinner with the table laid with things appropriate for 1805, as his grandson Simon Houfe has described in *Sir Albert Richardson The Professor*.

As well as writing his *Monumental Classic Architecture* (1914), he produced numerous articles and gave lectures on the neo-classical period, among them *The Empire Style in England*, which was published in *The Architectural Review* as early as 1911.

A comparison of the two sets of photographs gives a sense of the Professor growing into the house over the years as he was able to assemble suitable objects for it; but it is as if there was something proto-Modern about the relative bareness of the Saloon in 1922, when Randall Phillips said: 'There are no pictures in this room, yet one does not feel the want of them, the several mirrors (especially the long ones between the street windows, designed by Professor Richardson) and girandoles giving sufficient wall embellishment. A greenish grey carpet covers the floor, and grey, too is the colour of the walls, in contrast to which is the purple taffeta, with old-gold filigree used for the window hangings, and the yellow chenille of old French pattern used for some of the chair coverings . . . '

257 and 258. (Opposite) *The saloon in 1922 and 1934. The growth of a collection*

259. (Right) *The principal bedroom in 1934*

Gledstone Hall

YORKSHIRE

After the War Lutyens designed only two new large country houses, Gledstone, built between 1922 and 1926 for Sir Amos Nelson, and Middleton Park, in Oxfordshire, begun in 1934 and completed in 1938. As was said in the catalogue of the Lutyens exhibition in 1982, 'In all the classical schemes, Gledstone, the Washington Embassy, and finally Middleton Park, there is control and assurance that assumes a total mastery of the classical language that finds its greatest manifestation in the Roman Catholic Cathedral at Liverpool.' But it is the exterior, the setting and the circulation spaces that appear memorable at Gledstone, illustrated in *Country Life* on April 13 and 20, 1935, while the interiors seem a little disappointing. However the dining room is an interesting room, reworking the idea of the Marble Parlour at Houghton, which Lutyens also used in the Viceroy's House in Delhi.

260. *The dining room.*

Sudbury Hall

DERBYSHIRE

There were two probable reasons for *Country Life* returning to Sudbury for the articles published on June 15, 22 and 29, 1935. They were intended to record the improvements made by the 9th Lord Vernon and his wife, who had returned to live there in 1922. They re-arranged the house to great advantage, disguising the losses of the previous period, and they redecorated the drawing room in 'a pleasant May blue Hampton Court paper'. It is likely that the decision to publish the articles was also influenced by the discovery in the early 1930s of George Vernon's account book covering the building of the house, which provided dates and the identity of the craftsmen who had worked on its decoration. Thus it illustrates rather well the increasing role that research has come to play in writing about houses in *Country Life*, and its influence not only on the choice of houses but the way that they were approached.

261. *The saloon at Sudbury. Carving by Edward Pierce, plaster work by Bradbury and Pettifer, and ceiling painting by Laguerre*

Browsholme Hall

YORKSHIRE

Browsholme was already a great rarity when it was described in *Country Life* on July 13, 1935: a northern squire's house that had passed down from generation to generation for many centuries, preserving its special flavour of strength and remoteness. As Christopher Hussey wrote: 'Two hundred years ago, before the industrialisation of the north, there were many such old-fashioned conservative, intensely Royalist houses in the Dukedom and Earldom. Now few remain unaltered or in the hands of their original owners, if indeed the family retains a connection at all with its name-site. In all these respects Browsholme is an exception . . .' The Parkers descend from park keepers in the Forest of Bowland, on the spine of Lancashire and Yorkshire, and are recorded there in the late fourteenth century. However the sense of continuity and survival in the house owes a good deal to the antiquarian enthusiasms of Thomas Lister Parker, the friend of the first Lord de Tabley, the collector of contemporary British pictures, and Walter Fawkes, the patron of Turner, who succeeded in 1797: he played up its ancient character partly through the furniture and objects that he collected but also through introducing old fittings from elsewhere, like the panelling and overmantel in the library. At the same time, in 1805, he added on a new wing containing a drawing room designed by Jeffry Wyatt in what Christopher Hussey described as 'a singular blend of Soane and Tudor revival'. So today the house has the double fascination of a genuine old north country house overlayed with a subtle late eighteenth- and early nineteenth-century romanticism.

262. (Below) *The Wyatt drawing room*
263. (Opposite above) *The panelled library*
264. (Opposite below) *The kitchen with sheets of oatcake hanging on the line*

Bramshill

Hampshire

By the mid 1930s the uncertain future of country houses was becoming increasingly apparent, and thoughts were turning to what should be done to protect and preserve them. Naturally *Country Life* played a leading part in this, and the whole approach of Christopher Hussey to Bramshill, the great Jacobean house built by Lord Zouche and the seat of the Copes from 1699, is quite different from Tipping's on Hamilton Palace written some sixteen years before. In an article on its future published on August 17, 1935, he wrote 'When private tragedy is the cause of a public calamity, such as the sale of a great and historic family home undoubtedly is, words cannot express the pity.' He continued: 'It has been, and should in a rightly ordered world continue to be, a national possession; such a place that, did a foreigner ask to be shown a perfect example of the historic English home, one would take him to see. Rumours have indeed been current that the State contemplates its purchase intact for preservation . . . ' And he ended, 'The house, with 940 acres, is offered for sale in one lot with all its contents. . . . If Bramshill is not as it ought to be, acquired by the nation, at least it is to be hoped that a purchaser will come forward who will seize this unique opportunity for buying one of, say, the five supreme houses in England intact with all its wonderful things.' The house was, in fact, bought by the 2nd Lord Brocket that year, and in 1953 it was acquired by the Home Office for use as the Police Staff College, which it remains.

265. (Opposite above) *The great hall with its screen bearing the arms of Zouche*

266. (Opposite below) *Tapestries in the Great Drawing Room*

267. *The long gallery. The wainscot is grained to look like burr walnut*

Valewood

SURREY

This cottage is a suitable place to end, or rather break off, this survey of photographs from *Country Life*, because, as Christopher Hussey wrote on September 21, 1935: 'Actually the week-end cottage, as a genus, is in many ways more characteristic of our times than the country house itself.' Valewood was the kind of picturesque cottage that Shaw and Blomfield had drawn in the 1860s, and formed part of the background to Lutyens' early work. Oliver Hill found it in 1926 and Gertrude Jekyll helped him with the garden: 'With the house and farm buildings as a nucleus and the wooded Sussex valley as a background,' Christopher Hussey wrote, 'Mr Oliver Hill has created a little work of art, part garden and part sheer fairy story.' It may seem puzzling that while he was living there, he was pursuing the modern style in houses like Joldwynds, but, in fact, there was an underlying logic in that both express his 'zestful use of materials'. Christopher Hussey drew attention to the variety of objects in the house: 'a fantastic crew of carved wood figures of all ages and sizes, an astonishing assortment of hats, ship models and nautical gear, examples of Sussex ironwork, ancient and modern pottery, and quantities of glass. . . .' C.H. Reilly writing on Oliver Hill in *Scaffolding in the Sky* described how he filled his garden 'with every gay, amusing thing he has collected on his travels, even to a vast plaster bull by Manship painted vermillion which prances at one from the interior of a barn, as well as genuine cockatoos and monkeys', and how he dressed himself up when there 'in the strangest garments.' The walls of the parlour were 'hung with a white textile, the sofa covered with white canvas and with cushions of black and white skins or linen.'

It has a special interest for *Country Life*, because Christopher Hussey and Oliver Hill had become friends and indeed Christopher Hussey shared Valewood with him for five years until he married in 1936.

269. (Opposite above) *The hall. The colouring in browns and white was set by the zebra skin*
270. (Opposite below) *Draped fabric in the White Parlour*

268. *The Yellow Bedroom*

INDEX OF HOUSES

(Numerals in brackets are plate numbers)

Adcote 142–143 (116)
Allington Castle 28, 60 (9)
Ardenrun 54, 146–147 (32, 120, 121)
Avebury Manor 190–191 (176, 177)
Avenue House, Ampthill 252–253 (257, 258, 259)

Baddesley Clinton 14 (1)
Balmanno Castle 224–225 (217, 218)
Beaudesert 29, 180–181 (164, 165)
Beech House, Worthing 186–187 (170, 171, 172)
Belton House 52, 56, 111 (75)
Beningbrough 138, 212–213 (204, 205)
Berkeley Castle 234–235 (231, 232)
Blenheim Palace 136–137 (108, 109)
Blickling Hall 216–217 (208, 209)
Boughton House 135–136 (106, 107)
Bramshill 85, 258–259 (265, 266, 267)
Brinsop Court 51, 120, 160–161 (139, 140)
Brocket Hall 204 (195)
Browsholme Hall 256–257 (262, 263, 264)
Buscot Park 165 (145)
Buxted Park 28, 244–245 (244, 245)

Canons Ashby 48, 188–189 (173, 174, 175)
Castle Howard 9, 12, 208–209 (199, 200)
Chequers Court 17, 51, 144–145 (118, 119)
Chilham Castle 198–199 (187, 188)
Cliveden 153 (129)
Clouds 58, 116–117 (84, 85)
Cold Ashton Manor 28, 73, 200–201 (189, 190, 191)
Coleshill 56, 176–177 (158, 159, 160)
Crooksbury 42 (21)

Deanery Garden, Sonning 37, 44, 58, 92, 108–109 (14, 17, 72, 73)
Delhi, Viceroy's House 12, 35, 66, 232–233 (228, 229, 230)
Drakelowe Hall 99 (63)

Earlshall 52, 53, 120–121 (31, 88, 89, 90)
Erdigg 140–141 (113, 114, 115)

Gledstone Hall 12, 254 (260)
Godmersham 29 (12)
Groombridge Place 110 (74)

Haddo House 22 (5)
Haddon Hall 94–95 (57, 58)
Hamilton Palace 83, 173–175 (154, 155, 156, 157)
Hatfield House 15, 89 (51)
Herstmonceaux Castle 28, 168–169 (148, 149, 150)
Heveningham Hall 205 (196)
Hewell Grange 106–107 (70, 71)
High Glanau 51
High and Over 32, 77, 228–229 (13, 222, 223, 224)
High Cross Hill 79 (48)
Hill Hall 166–167 (146, 147)
Holme Lacy 26, 138–139 (110, 111, 112)
Houghton Hall 12, 129, 182–185 (100, 166, 167, 168, 169)
Hursley Park 132–133 (105, 106)

Iford Manor 131–132 (101, 102, 103)

Joldwynds 80, 250–251 (253, 254, 255, 256)

Kedleston Hall 158–159 (136, 137, 138)
Kelmarsh Hall 28 (11)
Kingston Lacy 114–115 (81, 82)
Knole 17, 150–151 (125, 126, 127)

Lindisfarne Castle 39, 44, 156–157 (19, 20, 133, 134, 135)
Little Ridge 152 (128)
London 42 Cheyne Walk 240–241 (238, 239, 240)
  Dorchester House 35, 83, 214–215 (206, 207)
  Holland House 119–120 (87)
  Home House 238–239 (235, 236, 237)
  11, Montagu Place 226 (219)
  Sir William Orpen's Studio 218–219 (210, 211, 212)
  15 Queen Anne's Gate 39, 47, 66 (27)
  11 Titchfield Place 226–227 (220,221)
Lyme Park 122–123 (91, 92, 93)

Mathern Palace 51, 143 (28, 29, 117)
Mottistone Manor 67 (40)
Mounton House 51, 162–163 (30, 141, 142, 143)
Munstead Wood 92–93, 108 (54, 55, 56)

Nether Lypiatt Manor 246–247 (246, 247, 248, 249)
Normanton 154–155 (130, 131, 132)
Nostell Priory 12, 58, 128 (2, 99)
Nymans 28, 236–237 (8, 233, 234)

Ockwells 112–113 (76, 77, 78, 79, 80)
Old Place, Lindfield 96–97 (59, 60, 61)
Orchards 98 (62)

Parham Park 28, 101 (10, 65)
Penheale Manor 66, 202–203 (192, 193, 194)
Plumpton Place 242–243 (35, 36, 241, 242, 243)
Port Lympne 192–193 (178, 179, 180)

Queen Mary's Dolls House 76, 194–197 (44, 181–186)
Quenby Hall 148–149 (122, 123, 124)

Raby Castle 164 (144)
Rufford Old Hall 63 (38, 39)

Sandringham 102–105 (Frontispiece, 66, 67, 68, 69)
Scotney Castle 65, 70, 72, 73 (42)
Sledmere 12, 15, 66, 68, 88, 170–171 (49, 50, 151, 152)
Snowshill Manor 210–211 (201, 202, 203)
Southill 220–221 (213, 214)
Sudbury Hall 118–119, 254–255 (86, 261)
Sutton Scarsdale 172 (153)
Sutton Place 90–91 (52, 53)

Treasurer's House, York 24, 26, 124–125 (94, 95, 96)
Trent Park 28, 230–231 (225, 226, 227)

Valewood 260–261 (45, 268, 269, 270)
Victoria and Albert Museum 24, 25, 26, 42, 47, 83, 99, 181 (6, 7)

Wardes 17, 178–179 (161, 162, 163)
Wardour Castle 222–223 (215, 216)
Welbeck Abbey 126–127 (97, 98)
Westwood Manor 28, 206–207 (197, 198)
Wentworth Woodhouse 248–249 (250, 251, 252)
Wilton House 100 (64)

GENERAL INDEX

(Numerals in brackets are plate numbers)

Architectural Review 20, 21, 22, 32, 33, 35, 36, 53, 108, 232

Batsford 20, 21, 25, 49
Bedford, Lemere 6, 132
Belcher, John and Macartney, Mervyn 20
Blomfield, Reginald 19, 20, 21, 35, 54, 67, 144, 166 (118)
Blow, Detmar 27, 152 (128)
Bodley and Garner 26, 106, 148 (70, 71)
Bolton, Arthur 12, 47, 58, 60, 69
Brierley, Walter 88, 170 (152)
Burlington Magazine 20, 53
Byron, Robert 35, 84, 232

Congreve, Lady 9, 39, 50
Connell, Amyas 32, 228 (13, 222, 223, 224)
Connoisseur, The 20, 22
Conway, Martin 60, 160, 162, 168, 178 (9)
Le Corbusier 31, 32, 77, 80
Cornish, C.J. 50, 52, 96
Country Life advertising 16, 17, 42, 168 (4)
books 21, 47, 49, 50, 51, 56, 57, 58, 61, 68, 69, 84, 108, 111
building 44, 46, 111 (22, 23, 24, 25, 26)
Dictionary of Furniture 24, 68, 69, 202
patronage 54, 56, 67, 68
photography 7, 8, 12, 13, 15, 20, 42, 49, 50, 63, 64, 65, 66, 94, 114, 123, 140, 205, 208, 222, 272 (18, 57, 81, 92, 196, 216)

Darwin, Bernard 6, 9, 13, 47, 84

Edwards, Ralph 9, 14, 24, 37, 61, 68, 69, 131, 202
Evans, Frederick 50, 61

Francis, E.C. 51, 162
Furniture, interest in 22, 23, 24, 25, 27, 47, 49, 124, 128, 138, 150, 186, 190, 191, 200, 202, 253

George, Ernest 24, 126, 131
Georgian Group 6, 35
Gill, Arthur 66, 232 (228, 229, 230)
Gotch, Alfred 20, 21, 49, 56, 72, 148, 189
Graham, Anderson 71, 157

Henson, A.E., 8, 13, 61, 62, 65, 66, 176, 208 (37, 38, 39, 158, 159, 160, 199, 200)

Hill, Oliver 32, 34, 35, 78, 79, 80, 160 (45, 47, 252, 254, 255, 256)
Hudson, Edward 6, 9, 13, 14, 15, 16, 17, 18, 22, 37, 39, 41, 42, 43, 46, 47, 49, 50, 53, 54, 60, 61, 62, 66, 67, 68, 92, 98, 108, 111, 143, 157, 194, 232, 242 (14, 15, 16, 17, 22–25, 27, 35, 36, 241–243)
Hussey, Christopher 6, 7, 9, 31, 32, 41, 47, 51, 56, 61, 65, 67, 69, 72, 73, 74, 75, 76, 77, 78, 79, 80, 81, 84, 85, 100, 120, 124, 194, 200, 208, 215, 216, 218, 220, 224, 226, 228, 230, 237, 240, 250, 256, 259, 260 (37, 41)

Jekyll, Gertrude 22, 37, 52, 54, 57, 61, 92, 98, 120, 194 (54, 55, 56)
Johnston, Philip Mainwaring 56, 57, 72, 178
Jourdain, Margaret 25, 26, 29, 32, 42, 47, 48, 49, 69, 140, 158, 172, 189, 244

Kitchen, Herbert 56, 57, 72
Knight, Frank and Rutley 16, 17 (4)
Knoblock, Edward 186, 226 (170–172, 219)

Latham, Charles 8, 15, 20, 21, 47, 49, 50, 51, 58, 69, 108 (52, 53)
Lee, Viscount Lee of Fareham 17, 60, 144 (118–119)
Lees-Milne 124, 191, 207
Lenygon 25, 26, 138, 212
Leyland, John 15, 50, 89
Lorimer, Sir Robert 27, 52, 53, 56, 92, 120, 224 (31, 88, 89, 90, 217, 218)
Lothian, Marquess of 36, 84, 85, 216 (208, 209)
Lutyens, Sir Edwin 6, 9, 12, 21, 27, 31, 32, 34, 35, 37, 39, 41, 43, 47, 53, 54, 56, 58, 67, 72, 73, 75, 92, 98, 108, 111, 116, 120, 143, 153, 157, 166, 194, 202, 232, 241, 254 (21, 22, 27, 35, 36, 54, 56, 72, 73, 91, 92, 93, 123, 133, 134, 135, 181–186, 228, 229, 230, 241, 242, 243, 260)
Lutyens, Barbara 157 (20)

Macquoid, Percy 9, 24, 26, 49, 68, 138, 194
Maude, Pamela 9, 39
Moore, Temple 26, 124
Morant 26, 138 (110)
Modern architecture and Movement 6, 19, 27, 29, 31, 32, 33, 34, 66, 77, 78, 79,

80, 81, 82, 85 (46, 47, 48, 222, 223, 224, 253, 254, 255, 256)
Muthesius 15, 19, 22, 37, 42, 98

Nash, Paul 60, 78 (34)
National Trust 6, 35, 36, 82, 85, 114, 124, 140, 144, 157, 189, 207, 210, 212, 216, 237
Newnes 13, 14, 17, 50
Newton, Ernest 54, 147 (32, 120, 121)

Oswald, Arthur 61, 79, 83, 84

Paget, Paul 67, 68 (40)
Pearson, Sir Neville 68
Peto, M.A. 24, 131, 165 (101, 102, 103)
Preservation thinking 35, 82, 83, 84, 85

Restoration 90, 94, 112, 120, 124, 131, 135, 143, 144, 148, 150, 157, 160, 168, 170, 180, 190, 200, 202, 207, 210, 224, 234, 246
Reilly, Sir Charles 9, 13, 35, 61, 66, 67, 260
Richardson, Sir Albert 21, 29, 210, 253 (257–259)
Riddell, Lord 13, 16, 17, 60, 66
Rouch, W.A. 15, 88 (49, 50)

Sassoon, Sir Philip 28, 29, 178, 192, 230 (178–180, 225–227)
Seely, John 67, 68 (40)
Shaw, J. Byam 15, 37 (3)
Sleigh, Frank 66
Summerson, Sir John 31, 35, 77, 176

Tedman, Arthur 66
Tilden, Philip 26, 178, 192 (178)
Tipping, H. Avray 6, 9, 22, 24, 25, 41, 49, 50, 52, 56, 57, 58, 60, 61, 68, 69, 71, 72, 73, 75, 120, 131, 138, 143, 145, 160, 162, 166, 168, 173, 176, 180, 181, 191, 208 (28, 29, 30, 41, 139, 141, 142, 143)
Triggs, Inigo 21, 22, 190

Ward 66
Weaver, Sir Lawrence 6, 9, 47, 52, 53, 54, 56, 58, 60, 61, 73, 77, 82, 120, 143, 147, 194
Wellesley, Lord Gerald 66, 73, 78, 186, 226 (220, 221)
Westley, F.W. 66 (151, 152)
Williams-Ellis, Sir Clough 35, 56